BOOKS FOR THE RETARDED READER

J. A. HART & J. A. RICHARDSON

UNITED KINGDOM EDITION
Prepared by J. A. HART

LONDON
ERNEST BENN LIMITED

This edition first published 1971
Ernest Benn Limited
Bouverie House, Fleet Street, London, EC4A 2DL

© *Joan A. Hart 1971*

Printed in Great Britain

ISBN 0 510-19630-6
Paperback 0 510-19631-4

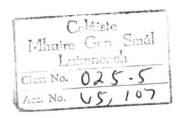

Contents

Acknowledgements

The authors wish to acknowledge their debt of gratitude to the late Sir Fred Schonell, one-time Vice-Chancellor of the University of Queensland, and to Professor G. Bassett, Dean of the Faculty of Education and Director of the Remedial Education Centre, University of Queensland, wherein much of the early work leading to the development of this publication took place.

They also wish to thank the editors of the *Slow Learning Child,* a journal published by the University of Queensland Press, for permission to use material which has appeared in the journal from time to time; the many publishers' agents and representatives who have provided much of the information; and Miss Merle O'Donnell who kindly made the assessment of the Trend series.

Preface
to the United Kingdom edition

'Books for the Retarded Reader' was first published in Australia in 1959. The period between the first edition and this present edition has been notable for an increasing interest in reading problems from a wide variety of disciplines outside education, and a considerable change in attitudes towards both reading disability and remedial teaching. Specific dyslexia has become almost a fashionable disease, surrounded by clouds of neurological speculation and endless discussion upon possible aetiology and the exact definition of terminology. Phonics have become respectable again and 'ITA' and 'Words in Colour' have their vociferous disciples. Elaborate teaching aids, workshops and laboratories promise improvement, if not cure, and teaching machines are beginning to proliferate.

But the problem of the child who finds it difficult to learn to read remains with us. Secondary schools continue to complain that a significant percentage of children coming up from the primary schools have inadequate reading skills to cope with secondary education. Child Guidance and Education Clinics have a constant stream of children requiring diagnosis and treatment of their learning problems. The world-wide eruption of parent pressure groups drawing attention to the educational needs of children suffering from 'Word Blindness', 'Specific Learning Difficulties' and other similar conditions emphasizes the gravity of the problem and a dissatisfaction with present facilities.

The uprising of public interest in reading disability is already having an appreciable effect. There is more research being carried out, remedial teaching and individual tutoring are increasing and there is a greater appreciation of the need for special materials for such children. Good teaching and good books remain the essential weapons in the fight against illiteracy. It is hoped that this book will provide a useful guide as to what is at present available to help such children and, through its inadequacies, indicate what is needed for the future.

The first and second Australian editions of the book were written by Professor J. Richardson, now of the Flinders University, South Australia and Mrs. J. Hart, now Clinical Psychologist, Royal Alexandra Hospital for Children, Sydney, N.S.W., in collaboration. The third and fourth Australian editions and the present United Kingdom edition have been edited and added to by Mrs. Hart alone, but follow closely the original work, adopting the format and detailed presentation which were devised jointly.

GENERAL PRINCIPLES FOR HELPING CHILDREN WITH READING DIFFICULTIES

Reading ability is a fundamental necessity in a modern community—the skill upon which our entire educational system is built. Although mass media of communication such as radio and television play an increasing role in life, they are unlikely to supersede written communication entirely, with the result that illiteracy remains a severe handicap in our culture.

Fries (1962)[1] describes language as the storehouse of human experience, pointing out that the development of written language has increased the storage capacity by allowing communication with writers outside the limits of time and space. Through books we have access to scholarship and wisdom accrued through many centuries of human experience which would be otherwise lost to us. Any adult without a reasonable competence in reading must be regarded as culturally deprived.

Reading is a complex process closely related to both listening and speaking. The process of receiving a message through *talk* can be described as making a meaning response to the oral signals of a language code. For example, if a speaker says 'chair', the sound heard by the listener is the oral signal in the English language code for a common object in the environment. The listener responds by knowing which particular object is referred to. Such oral signals are transmitted to the nervous system by sound vibrations impinging on the ear. Similarly, in reading, the reader responds to visual signals for the same language code, in this case transmitted to the nervous system by light vibrations reaching the eye. Reading is thus a form of linguistic activity dependent upon the language control achieved by the potential reader. It is impossible to make meaningful responses to unfamiliar language signals. This is accepted by authors of children's books, who endeavour to simplify vocabulary and syntax, and choose objects and situations within the comprehension of the books' likely readers. It is important to emphasize that responding to printed signals—*barking at print* by uttering certain sounds—is not reading unless a meaningful response is made at the same time. Unless this is done, ideas are not transmitted and communication does not take place.

A child learning to read has to accomplish the transfer from interpreting language signals represented by auditory patterns to that of interpreting graphic patterns, a process requiring intensive practice and one that has led to the development of complex teaching procedures and methods. But most children make this transition without difficulty, some even apparently learning to read without any outside help. It is the retarded reader who fails to establish this automatic habit and thus fails to find meaning in written symbols. Such readers are distributed on a continuum from those who have failed completely to make the transfer from sound to graphic symbol to those who have mastered the process but who are so slow that all their effort is taken up with the mechanical translation so that they tend to lose the meaning. All such children need special help if they are to achieve functional literacy. Treatment will involve psychological assessment, special teaching techniques, exercises and apparatus, all aimed at helping the child to interpret the many graphic signs in his environment. In such treatment, the most important materials are books, and it is essential that the most suitable for the purpose are chosen.

The main purpose of 'Books for the Retarded Reader' is that of making an analysis of available material for those children unable to make profitable use of normal school texts. The selection includes both books written specifically for this purpose and those, written originally for other uses, which have proved helpful in remedial work. No book has been included which has not been thought by the editor to be valuable in some capacity, even though it may have some aspects which may be open to criticism.

With the continued expansion of secondary education, the need, not only for specific reading and English usage books, but of appropriate social studies and science texts increases. Therefore, special sections concerned with materials for retarded pupils in secondary schools have been included. Selection is limited by considerations of space, but it is hoped that the series chosen will give some indications of both what is needed and what is available.

CATEGORIZATION AND DIAGNOSIS OF BACKWARD READERS

Adequate remedial treatment is impossible without individual diagnosis of a child's difficulties and assessment of his intellectual, social and emotional potential. Vernon (1962)[2] divided poor readers into moderate cases due mainly to environmental causes, emotionally maladjusted cases, and severe cases or *dyslexics* with possibly some organic or constitutional factor. This division is useful when considering the aetiology of the disability, but from the teaching point of view Early's (1963)[3] classification on the basis of the type of treatment needed is possibly more useful. She suggests three classes:

1. **Remedial cases.** This includes children with gross discrepancies between their performance in reading and their intellectual capacity as

assessed by intelligence tests and performance in other fields. These children have been described variously by such terms as 'word blind', 'dyslexic', 'suffering from minimal cerebral dysfunction', and recently as 'having multiple minimal handicaps' (Wertheim, 1967)[4]. Hypotheses are still being put forward to account for such gross reading retardation including a bio-chemical theory by Smith and Carrigan (1959)[5], a neuro-physical approach by Delacato (1963)[6] and a neurological theory by Macdonald Critchley (1964)[7]. So far, no totally valid explanation has been put forward, although there is evidence of physiological, developmental and constitutional factors in some cases. *The Illinois Test of Psycholinguistic Abilities* (Kirk and McCarthy, 1961)[8] makes possible the assessment of a child's language development in areas presumed to be related to reading ability and recent research has shown that remedial programmes based on ITPA profiles have significant effects on reading improvement (Hart, 1963, Outridge, 1964, Appelt, 1965)[9]. *The Marion Frostig Developmental Test of Visual Perception* (Frostig et al. 1964)[10] enables a detailed examination to be made of associated visual-perceptual skills which are relevant to the reading process. Evidence obtained from such examinations is critical in diagnosis of difficulties and the planning of remediation. Children requiring such intensive investigation are usually referred to Child Guidance Clinics and need careful, long-term retraining. Even then, prognosis in many cases is doubtful and many achieve only a limited literacy.

2. **Corrective cases.**   This category includes children who have fallen sufficiently behind their peers in reading to make it difficult for them to keep up with their class work, even though their intellectual capacity is comparable with their classmates. Generally there is a fairly clearly identifiable syndrome of causes for such retardation, although it may become overlaid with a reactive emotional disturbance if the child is made to feel he has failed to live up to teacher or parental expectations. Causative factors include:

a. prolonged absence from school;
b. frequent short absences from school;
c. frequent school changes, or changes from one county or country to another;
d. bilingualism;
e. late diagnosis of minor physical handicaps, such as poor sight or partial deafness, allergic ailments and asthma, and speech defects;
f. immaturity, frequently combined with too early a start on formal class work;
g. poor quality early teaching and the effect of large classes;

h. unfavourable parental attitudes such as over-protection, lack of interest or unrealistic expectations;
i. sibling rivalries and unfavourable comparison with brighter members of the family;
j. poor motivation and lack of application, inattentiveness and restlessness;
k. traumatic experiences and minor emotional disturbances including separation anxiety on starting school and reaction to unsympathetic teacher handling;
l. poor cultural background and lack of appropriate pre-school experience.

Richardson (1957),[11] in an analysis of one hundred cases of reading retardation, showed that in only a minority of cases could the retardation be regarded as due to a single adverse circumstance but was typically due, in his sample, to a combination of circumstances, a finding substantiated by many later workers.

Such children can frequently be successfully treated within the school, either by a suitably trained member of the staff, assisted by school guidance officers or visiting educational psychologists, or by itinerant specialist teachers. Treatment should be undertaken on a short-term basis and can be intensive. The children need not be withdrawn from their regular class work except for the periods when they receive their special help. It can be anticipated that many such children will eventually regain their class level of achievement or at least attain a practical literacy. The teacher will be unlikely to be able to treat directly many of the causative factors, but knowledge of them makes for sympathy and understanding, which may in turn lead to the establishment of good relationships and an increased motivation to learn.

3. **Developmental cases.**   This category includes children with all-round deficiency in academic ability; that is, those making low scores on verbal intelligence tests and who fail in normal schools. Such readers are usually found in schools for the educationally sub-normal and in the bottom ten per cent of primary and lower secondary classes. Their rate of progress is determined by their lack of ability, so it is necessary for them to have special educational attention throughout their school life if they are to make maximum use of their limited potential. Unless the low level of general ability is combined with a severe language disability, sensory weakness or poor perceptual development, there is generally no reason why such children should not learn to read, although their progress will tend to be slow and the developmental extent less than for children of higher intellectual capacity.

COMMON FACTORS NECESSARY TO SUCCESS
IN REMEDIAL TEACHING

On surveying the literature on teaching reading to slow-learning children of all types, it becomes apparent that, with corrective and developmental cases, many different methods have been tried and shown to be successful, particularly when used under the supervision of their originators. This suggests that, whatever the method, there are certain essential factors that underlie all successful remedial teaching. They appear to come under the following headings:

Understanding the Individual Child

The recognition of individual differences is of primary importance. Remedial teachers need detailed knowledge of their pupils; it is essential to be aware not only of reading difficulty but also of physical and emotional weakness, personal idiosyncrasies and home and educational background. This makes possible the planning of individual programmes and the establishment of good teacher-pupil relationships which are vital with discouraged and failing children.

Adequate Diagnosis of Difficulties

This follows immediately from above. Diagnosis necessary for effective remedial teaching must include sufficient information to allow tentative allocation into one of the above categories of retarded readers. It should be carried out by a suitably qualified and experienced psychologist and supplemented by the teacher's own observations. An estimate of the child's general intellectual capacity must be obtained from tests and his level of function from objective attainment tests and school reports; his attainment levels in the main aspects of reading must be established and an analysis made of his language and perceptual skills. Attainment levels can be obtained by using such tests as those of Schonell (1962)[12] and the Neale Analysis of Reading Ability (1958)[13]. Objective results can be expanded by observations of the child's method of attack on new words not immediately recognized, his mastery of phonics, and evidence of reversals, distortions and lack of comprehension. Initial diagnosis is of necessity incomplete and must be rounded out in the light of the teacher's experience with the child. Diagnosis is only valuable in the initial stages if the teacher makes use of the information obtained as a basis for selecting methods and materials. It is pointless obtaining a careful diagnosis and then using one's favourite method of teaching reading, regardless of whether it is suitable for the child or not.

The Necessity for Immediate Success

The retarded child frequently experiences failure and discouragement over a number of years and may suffer a loss of confidence not only in his ability to cope with school work but in himself altogether. He is then a psychological as well as an educational problem. The re-establishment of his self-respect is an immediate and major task for the teacher. Ensuring the initial success is an integral part of any remedial method, as it represents the beginning of rehabilitation. Instruction should take place in a friendly, permissive atmosphere and be so geared to a child's attainment level that he can manage what is required of him without difficulty. It should move forward in very easy stages with many pauses for consolidation and revision, and there should be clearly-defined, short-term goals such as the acquiring of twenty new sight words, the completion of a short book, or the reading of a short passage without error or hesitation. As confidence and skills increase, the goals set may become more exacting and the period required to reach them extended. But goals should never be unrealistic or set too far away in time. Some means should be provided of giving tangible evidence of success, such as progress charts, graphs of increased speed of reading, *before and after* tape recordings and lists of completed books. Suitable rewards can provide added reinforcement.

Praise and encouragement should be given freely for effort and relative achievement rather than for actual level of attainment. The child's improvement should be measured in relation to his attainment level and rate of progress prior to remedial teaching, never by comparison with other members of his peer group and siblings. Because he is used to discouragement and at least implied censure for failure, an opportunity to succeed, even to a limited extent, may have pronounced therapeutic effect.

It is preferable to use an unfamiliar approach, with books and materials that are novel to the pupil. This avoids reminder of earlier failure, boredom with previously used books of unsuitable interest level, and comment from classmates that the child with reading difficulties has to go back to books already mastered by the others. The method chosen should build on such strengths as the child already possesses, rather than to attempt to bolster up weaknesses in the beginning. Specific training in perception and language development can be carried on concurrently, and the remediation of specific reading difficulties such as reversals or poor discrimination can be undertaken once confidence has been built up. Early success is more likely if the child's interests can be taken into account when choosing books and exercises. The dullest child finds it easier to acquire a sight vocabulary if he is personally concerned with the subject he is reading about.

The Attitude of the Teacher

In most cases, it is not the method of teaching which contributes most to the child's improvement, but the efforts of the teacher himself. He must really believe in the child's ability to improve and that what he is doing is worthwhile. Without this, as recent studies of teachers' expectations as determinants of pupils' intellectual competence carried out in America (Rosenthal and Jacobson, 1968)[14] have shown, success is unlikely. With belief in the child's ultimate ability to succeed, method can take second place. This accounts for the quite often extraordinary success rates reported by people using special methods that they have devised themselves.

Remedial Reading as Part of a Wider Rehabilitation Process

In some ways the most important consideration for the remedial teacher is the realization that improvement in reading is only part of the therapeutic process. Schonell (1961)[15] points out that:

> The reading programme for backward readers must be intimately linked with a reorientation of their whole school programme. They must be provided with plenty of opportunities for expressing themselves and thus regain their lost self-esteem and diminished self-confidence. That is, not only their reading lessons but the whole of their school work must be planned on therapeutic lines.

Such a re-orientation is easier to establish in ESN schools with smaller classes and a less stringent academic programme. In the normal primary school, it presupposes a close co-operation between class and remedial teacher, careful planning and a flexible approach. Ideally, it would mean complete individualization of teaching programmes for the child in difficulties. In practice, it is limited to a deep understanding by both class and remedial teachers of the child's educational and emotional problems and a constant willingness to encourage, to make allowances, to adapt and to give opportunities for successful completion of tasks.

As many of the collateral causes of the child's difficulties are often outside the school, treatment such as has been suggested may not be completely effective and other action may be necessary which may be outside the competence of the teacher. If, for instance, there are handicapping factors in the home situation, the school can do little to help directly. But other agencies, such as child guidance clinics, school health services and family-service units may be involved. When this is so, both class and remedial teacher should be aware of the agency's activities as they affect the pupil and should endeavour to co-operate where possible. In other cases, direct contact with the parents of children whose school failure seems at least partially due to external factors, to discuss the child's educational development rarely fails to be a valuable experience for all concerned. Frank discussion of the child's learning difficulties may lead to better understanding of his total needs by both parents and teacher. In many cases, success or failure in remedial teaching is dependent upon the degree of parental understanding and support which has been secured in this way.

On a more practical level, many parents are grateful for suggestions for helping their child at home. This can be one way of ensuring that a child gets the necessary supervised extra reading practice, without nagging, criticism or over emphasis on scholastic achievement. At the same time, involving the parents actively in the treatment leads in many cases to a clearer understanding of their children's problems and potentialities, resulting frequently in healthier family relationships and a general release from tension.

ESSENTIAL QUALITIES NECESSARY IN BOOKS FOR RETARDED READERS

Children who have failed to learn to read at the same time as their peers tend to develop negative attitudes towards books. Reading is included among those activities to be avoided at all costs because they show up the child's limitations. To obtain the interest of such a child, he must be convinced that books have something to offer that is worth the hard work that learning to read entails. This is no easy task, as the books offered have to compete with the facile attractions of television and the cinema and the easy way out provided by comic strips. And the older the pupil, the harder the task becomes! To be suitable for remedial teaching, books for retarded readers must satisfy the following criteria:

1. They must be immediately acceptable to the potential reader, having neither a babyish nor dull appearance and giving no external evidence of having been written specifically for failing readers.

2. The books must be suitable for the pupil with regard to both level of reading difficulty and interest level of subject matter. As the interests of retarded children remain close to those of normal children of equivalent chronological age, rather than being appropriate to their mental age or attainment levels, it is important to find books for them in which the interest level remains high whilst the reading difficulty is much lower.

3. The books should be written in simple English conforming to generally accepted English literary usage, with a minimum of slang and colloquialisms

yet at the same time using vocabulary, syntax and structure which are within the language control and experience of those likely to read them.

4. They should be well produced with spacious layouts, with clear, plain printing of at least 12pt. type and well illustrated. The use of colour adds to the immediate attraction of the books.

THE PURPOSE OF THIS BOOKLIST

The aim of this publication is to provide a means by which people who are trying to help children with reading difficulties can obtain an overall view of what is available and from the books listed choose the ones most suitable for their particular pupils. Such people include teachers of normal classes in both primary and secondary schools, teachers in special schools for physically and mentally handicapped children and for those with sensory defects, remedial teachers and parents who are trying to give their children help at home.

For the Teacher of the Normal Class

Most classes in both primary and secondary schools show a wide range of reading ability among pupils and generally include at least a few pupils whose reading skills are inadequate for their class level either in all aspects of the subject or in some particular basic skill. The reading material provided for the class is likely to be quite unsuitable for this unfortunate minority; neither will they be able to read their subject texts. Yet it is undesirable to go back to books provided for earlier classes as, quite apart from the social stigma this would represent, such books would be too immature in approach to appeal to such pupils; and, in any case, most of them will have already experienced failure when using such books earlier in their school life. Such material would certainly not be conducive to changing defeatist attitudes and re-establishing confidence in relation to reading.

The present list provides a wide selection of books ranging from adventure stories to science textbooks, with interest levels ranging from those of children in early primary school to those of school leavers and young adults. All of them have comparatively low levels of reading difficulty with respect to vocabulary, sentence structure and amount of help to be derived from the illustrations. The list makes it possible for the teacher who is not a reading specialist to choose the most suitable books available even if he is unable to have close contact himself with bookshops and libraries, and it helps to prevent waste of limited resources on unsuitable material. For instance, children placed in a small remedial group within the classroom can be provided with appropriate books for their abilities—books which are at the same time attractive enough to appeal to the average child as supplementary reading—so that there is no question of the rest of the class looking down on the slow learners who are using such books.

A further advantage is that many of the recommended books are carefully graded in difficulty and have accompanying workbooks. This allows the more backward children to work at their own pace, independently. They will then no longer require the almost undivided attention of the class teacher during the reading period in order to be gainfully occupied.

For the Remedial and Special Class Teacher

In remedial classes made up of children with weakness in some or all of the basic subjects and in special schools and classes for the mentally and physically handicapped, grouping for reading may well be based on reading achievement as assessed by standardized reading tests rather than on a class basis. Books and materials can then be selected from the list accordingly. For a remedial class in a primary school and for the various types of special schools, pupils can be divided roughly into three reading levels as follows:

Group 1. Children with reading ages over 8.0 years.
Group 2. Children with reading ages between 6.5 and 8.0 years.
Group 3. Those virtually non-readers whose attainment age on the tests is less than 6.5 years.

These large divisions can then be subdivided as is practical, according to age, sex and interests.

Children in Group 1, which includes most retarded readers found in secondary schools, consist of those who mastered the basic reading skills but have not made the break-through to absolute literacy, understanding and the transmission of ideas through the printed page. They have neither fluency nor speed and frequently consider reading a drudgery rather than a pleasure. It is possible to provide such children with a wide variety of reading experiences suited to their ages from almost all sections of this book. Many suggestions for improving comprehension, increasing word-recognition skills and other associated activities will be found in Section 9, 'Books for the Teacher' (p. 95) and in the various workbooks and books on basic English usage. Programmes planned from such material will enable the pupils to work independently for some periods, freeing the teacher to give more attention to less advanced children.

Pupils in the middle group (Group 2) have usually started to read simple books but have made little progress towards independence in word-recognition. Frequently, they have reasonable sight vocabularies, but have failed to acquire techniques of word analysis and sound synthesis, and the means of using phonics and syllabification as aids to further progress. They are the group that demands perhaps the greatest share of the teacher's time, for they derive little satisfaction from silent reading and need frequent short periods of oral reading in small supervised groups. The carefully graded series in Sections 1 and 3, whichever is the most suited to the age of the pupils, will be the basic means of giving help. Such oral practice should be followed by group vocabulary study and the silent preparation of the passage to be read, and should be supplemented by phonic drills, word building practice, exercises encouraging the use of contextual clues and training in improving the understanding of what is read. Children in this group frequently benefit from individual attention to specific weaknesses, such as a marked tendency to reversals, and weakness in visual and aural discrimination. Suggestions for such treatment are to be found in Schonell (1961)[16], Bond and Tinker (1957)[17] and Tansley (1967)[18] and in many other of the books suggested in Section 9. Programmes in language development and in training visual-perceptual skills can be carried on concurrently as part of the whole remedial programme.

The third group needs active pre-reading programmes before they are ready for formal reading instruction, emphasizing either language or visuo-perceptual skills, whichever seems to be the pupil's greatest need. A completely new start in reading is also needed using stimulating material and working from their strengths towards their weaknesses—i.e. a child with good visual skills but poor auditory skills will be more likely to succeed by a 'look-and-say' method, leaving the acquiring of phonic values until he has made some progress, whilst the child with faulty visual perception may do better with a phonic method. Choice depends on the diagnosis of specific difficulties. In a large class, such children are a considerable problem in organization as they require individual attention and find it difficult to work on their own for more than short periods.

For the Parents of the Retarded Reader

This list should also be an asset to the parent attempting to help his own child with reading problems. It describes books that will be, in the main, different from those he uses habitually at school and provides details as to difficulty level, age suitability and price that will aid inexperienced persons to choose books in keeping with a particular child's age and capabilities. Perhaps, too, it will be a help to booksellers' assistants, who are frequently asked to help find suitable material and have little else to guide them. Misled by attractive illustrations, presentation, subject matter, his own childhood recollections, and sometimes by the ill-judged enthusiasm of the salesman, a parent may find it woefully easy to choose books that are too difficult both in reading level and content for the child for whom they are intended. Then the books stay on the shelf gathering dust whilst the child resorts to 'reading' comics and misses the essential experience of finding pleasure in books.

A SIMPLE REMEDIAL READING LESSON

With the ever-present shortage of trained remedial teachers, it frequently falls to the lot of parents without teaching experience and secondary school teachers without specific training beyond their own subjects to endeavour to help the failing child. It therefore seems appropriate to provide an outline of a simple individual reading lesson. This may be of help in planning remedial programmes and can be varied according to each child's particular needs. These basic principles must be stressed:

1. Short regular periods are essential if progress is to be made and the child's enthusiasm maintained. The ideal is half an hour every day.

2. The child who is backward in reading has necessarily missed many of the language experiences enjoyed by others of his age. He needs, more than anything else, as much practice as possible with interesting books that are well within the compass of his limited skills. He also needs to be read to regularly for short periods, to help improve his vocabulary and knowledge of structure, to teach him what reading is all about and to whet his appetite for more, so that he will be ready to try on his own.

3. The reading lesson should be a pleasant experience for both parties, not a form of torture for pupil and teacher. The teacher, parent or no, must be encouraging and permissive, praising for effort rather than performance, pointing out errors without criticism for failure and doing his best to motivate the child into trying to become independent. If tempers get frayed easily, or either pupil or teacher becomes upset over home lessons, it is better to give up the attempt and find someone outside the family and less emotionally involved to give the necessary help.

Regular, individual reading periods at home or school should not exceed forty minutes in length and should be divided roughly as follows:

1. Ten to fifteen minutes oral reading from a carefully graded reader with a controlled vocabulary selected according to the child's present level of instruction, i.e. at the level at which he has difficulty with about five per

cent of the total running vocabulary of the book. The teacher remains on the alert to supply any unknown word so that the continuity of the story is not broken, but encourages the child to use context clues, initial letters and familiar syllables as aids to recognition.

2. Following the oral reading, approximately ten minutes can be taken up with the child doing simple exercises based on what he has read and testing his comprehension of the story. These should be of the *missing word* or *multiple choice* type, involving the maximum of silent reading with the minimum of writing. It is helpful to choose a reading scheme in which such activities are provided within the books or in accompanying workbooks.

3. Some form of word recognition drill occupies the next ten minutes. With younger children, words can be printed on cards and practice given in immediate recognition. The child also copies such words, which should be chosen from those he failed to read during oral practice, into his notebook two or three times, or traces them as a further aid to learning. Word cards can be kept in a special box divided into sections labelled 'Known' and 'Not Known' and provide a visible means of assessing progress. Regular revision periods should be given. With older children, word lists kept in a special book can replace the cards.

As the child improves, sight vocabulary drill, except for a few irregular words, can be replaced by word-building activities using words such as 'and', 'up', etc. as basic units. The words built up should be limited in number and should only include those in common use.

4. The lesson should close with ten to fifteen minutes silent reading by the child for enjoyment only. The books chosen should be slightly below the child's actual reading level, so that he can read them with ease, and should be quite short, so that he can have the pleasant experience of completing the story quickly and easily.

Experienced teachers will recognize the above plan as unsophisticated and 'first-aid' only. The child who fails to improve under such a regimen needs complete diagnosis and expert help.

REFERENCES

1. Fries, C. C. *Linguistics and Reading.* New York, Holt, Rinehart and Winston, Inc.,1962.
2. Vernon, M. D. 'Specific Dyslexia', *Br. Journ. Ed. Psych.* 32, 2, 1962.
3. Early, M. 'Teaching Reading to Slow Learners in Secondary Schools', *Slow Learning Child,* 10, 2, 1963.
4. Wertheim, E. S. 'The School Age Child with Multiple Minimal Handicaps', *Aus. Paediatric Journ.,* 3, 1, 1967.
5. Smith, D. and Carrigan, P. *The Nature of Reading Disability.* New York, Harcourt Brace, 1959.
6. Delacato, C. H. *Diagnosis and Treatment of Speech and Language Problems.* Illinois, C. A. Thomas, 1963.
7. Critchley, M. *Developmental Dyslexia.* London, Heinemann Medical Books, 1964.
8. Kirk, S. A. and McCarthy, J. *Examiners Manual, Illinois Test of Psycholinguistic Abilities: Experimental Edition.* University of Illinois Press, 1961.
9. Hart, N., Outridge, M. and Apelt, W. 'Summary of Studies Carried Out by Staff Members of the Guidance and Special Education Branch, Education Department, Queensland', *Bulletin for Psychologists,* No. 6, February, 1967.
10. Frostig, M. et al. *Developmental Test of Visual Perception. Rev. Ed* Palo Alto, Consulting Psychologists Press, 1966.
11. Richardson, J. A. *'Causes of Reading Retardation in Primary Schools'.* Unpublished Ph.D. thesis, University of Queensland, 1957.
12. Schonell, F. J. and Schonell, F. E. *Diagnostic and Attainment Testing, fourth edition.* Edinburgh, Oliver and Boyd, 1962.
13. Neale, M. D. *Neale Analysis of Reading Ability.* London, Macmillan, 1958.
14. Rosenthal, R. and Jacobson, L. 'Self-fulfilling Prophecies in the Classroom: Teachers' Expectations as Unintended Determinants of Pupils' Intellectual Competence', in Deutsch, M, Katz, I and Jensen, A. R. (Eds.) *Social Class, Race and Psychological Development.* New York, Holt, Rinehart and Winston, Inc., 1968.
15. Schonell, F. J. *The Psychology and Teaching of Reading.* Edinburgh, Oliver and Boyd, 1942.
16. Schonell, F. J. *Backwardness in the Basic Subjects.* Edinburgh, Oliver and Boyd, 1942.
17. Bond, G. L. and Tinker, M. A. *Reading Difficulties: Their Diagnosis and Correction.* New York, Appleton, Century, Crofts, 1957.
18. Tansley, A. E. *Reading and Remedial Reading.* London, Routledge and Kegan Paul, 1967.

ARRANGEMENT OF SECTIONS AND BASIS OF CLASSIFICATION

For ease of reference, the books have been classified under nine headings as follows:

Section 1.   Reading Schemes for Older Backward Pupils

This includes those series written specifically for teaching pupils over nine years old the basic skills necessary for functional literacy. In spite of their simplicity, controlled vocabulary and careful construction, they have a high interest level and their subject matter is appropriate for the age of the pupils likely to be using them.

Section 2.   Supplementary Reading Material for Older Pupils

This lists those graded series and other sets of readers suitable for providing extra reading experience for pupils using the materials suggested in Section 1.

Section 3.   Introductory Reading Schemes Suitable for Younger Retarded Readers

This section includes both series written especially for children starting to learn to read at seven years or later and a selection of infant reading schemes which have proved useful in remedial work.

Section 4.   Supplementary Reading Material for Younger Children

Included here are simple books which will amuse and interest young children with very limited reading skills and thus provide them with necessary extra practice.

Section 5.   School Library Books: Adventure and Other Stories

Most of the books listed here are not primarily written for poor readers but rather with the needs of the non-academic child in mind. They all have a mature interest level and many would be helpful in classes for adults with limited reading ability.

Section 6.   School Library Books: Interests and Activities

This section lists many semi-technical books, written in simple language, which will appeal to the pupil with few scholastic ambitions but who enjoys practical and concrete occupations. Many of these books would make useful class reference texts in ESN schools.

Section 7.   Books for Teaching Essential Reading Skills, Spelling and Basic English Usage

In this section there are conventional English schemes written in simple language that makes them suitable for the poorer reader and also series designed for teaching particular reading skills such as phonic analysis, word structure and improved comprehension.

Section 8.   Books on Social Studies and Science

These books have usually been written as introductory tests for use in primary schools, but have been chosen because they combine simplicity of style and language with a sufficiently mature approach to make them acceptable and useful to older pupils who would not have sufficient reading skill to use the texts normally provided.

Section 9.   Books for the Teacher

A few of the most valuable of the many books and manuals on the teaching and psychology of reading, and on special education and mental retardation generally, are listed here with a brief indication of their contents. It is hoped that they will provide a starting point for teachers wishing to extend their technical skills in the field of reading improvement and to widen their knowledge of educational retardation in general.

These sections are by no means discrete and there is considerable overlapping of their contents as a particular series can frequently appeal to a very wide range of children. Also individuals vary widely in the maturity of their interests. Except in Section 9, where the books have been listed alphabetically, the books and series have been arranged in order of increasing reading difficulty (to make it easier to find the book most suitable for a particular pupil or class).

REVIEWS

The decision on what essential details should be given concerning each book was made after reference to reports on research into the question of what constitutes the *readability* of any text. Such work, mainly carried out in the

United States of America, was summarized by Dale and Chall (1949)[1] who suggested that the most relevant factors appear to be as follows:

1. *typographical details,* such as style and size of type, page layout, width of margins, paper and use of colour;

2. *interest* of the contents, which covers the liveliness of the story and characterization, the action involved and the element of surprise introduced;

3. *style of expression* which takes in vocabulary difficulty, sentence and paragraph structure and other expressional elements.

Most of these factors are specifically commented on in the reviews, together with comments on purpose and suitability of each book or series. An estimate of the *readability* or difficulty of each book or series is given in terms of reading age (RA); the higher the estimated reading age, the more difficult the book is considered. It would have been possible to express the difficulty level in terms of class or grade level, but not only does this differ from place to place, but also most standardized reading tests are scored in terms of reading age. It seemed appropriate to regard the reading age of a book as roughly equivalent to the score on a standardized test that would be made by a child who was capable of reading the book without difficulty. Consideration was given to the possibility of computing a readability index from formulae such as those put forward by Flesch (1948)[2], Dolch (1951)[3], or Spache (1958)[4] but they are tedious to apply and do not correlate highly with each other or with subjective estimates of reading difficulty. McLeod (1962)[5] suggested that the criteria on which such formulae are based are themselves subjective. Dolch, for instance, accepts the publisher's grade designation as a criterion of difficulty level. McLeod has shown that an empirical approach to the assessment of book readability is possible, but his method has too many practical difficulties to allow general application.

It has been decided, therefore, to estimate reading difficulty by comparing each book with the generally accepted reading level of the Happy Venture Readers (Schonell and Sergeant, 1938)[6] and the Wide Range Readers (Schonell and Flowerdew, 1951)[7] which are as follows:

Happy Venture Readers		*Wide Range Readers*	
	RA	Blue or Green	RA
Introductory Book } Book 1	5-6	Book 1	7-7½
		Book 2	7½-8
Book 2	6-6½	Book 3	8-8½
Book 3	6½-7	Book 4	8½-9
Book 4	7-7½	Book 5	9-10
		Book 6	10-11

The assessment of maturity or interest age (IA) of the books takes into account subject matter, style of production, illustrations and length. It is only a rough guide, as no account can be taken of the wide individual differences that are likely to be found in the tastes and interests of pupils. It is a purely subjective estimate based on the editor's experience as a remedial teacher and psychologist in Great Britain, Queensland and New South Wales.

As well as estimates of reading and interest age, the following information is given about each series selected:

Price. The prices quoted are the United Kingdom retail prices, as supplied by the publishers or their agents between January and June 1970. Such prices are subject to alteration and should be regarded as merely a guide to comparative cost.

Covers. It was decided that information concerning the type of covers, their durability and attractiveness, should be included as an aid to those teachers who are unable to inspect books personally before purchasing them.

Printing. A rating is given which includes both clarity of appearance and suitability of type size and general page layout. In many cases, qualitative comments are added. Each book is rated for printing as follows:

excellent	indicates outstanding production, style, choice of type face and page layout;
good	indicates clear printing, well-chosen type and good layout;
fair	indicates adequate but not outstanding printing and below average page layout.

The size of type face is also included to give the teacher some idea of the appearance of the printing. Specimens of each type size are given in an appendix at the end of the book.

Illustrations. Details are given of the frequency, style appeal and motivation value; also of method of reproduction.

Vocabulary. The term 'controlled' is used in the technical sense of indicating rigid limitation of vocabulary and regular, frequent repetition of all words used, in a variety of contexts. Vocabulary is usually carefully chosen with regard to the language development of the potential user. 'Restricted vocabulary' is used to indicate that an attempt has been made to limit the difficulty level of the vocabulary and the number of word classes used in any particular book. 'Graded' implies a gradual increase (throughout a series of books) in the number and difficulty of words introduced.

24

Comments are also made under this heading on the complexity of sentence structure and literary style.

Appraisal. This usually includes some indication of the anticipated usefulness of the book or series, and gives brief comments on the subject matter, the approach to reading chosen by the author and the likely appeal that the books will have for backward readers. A selection of representative titles is included to give examples of coverage. The authors and publishers are also given, beside the title of the series.

REFERENCES

1.   Dale, E. and Chall, J. S. 'The Concept of Readability' in Dale, E. (Ed.), *Readability,* USA, 1949.
2.   Flesch, R. 'A New Readability Yardstick'. *Journ. Applied Psych.,* 32, 3, 1948.
3.   Dolch, E. *Teaching Primary Reading.* Illinois, Garrard Press, 1951.
4.   Spache, G. *Good Reading for Poor Readers.* Illinois, Garrard Press, 1958.
5.   McLeod, J. 'Estimation of Readability of Books of Low Difficulty', *Br. Journ Ed. Psych.,* 32, 2, 1962.
6.   Schonell, F. J. and Sergeant, I. *Happy Venture Readers.* Edinburgh, Oliver and Boyd, 1938.
7.   Schonell, F. J. and Flowerdew, P. *Wide Range Readers.* Edinburgh, Oliver and Boyd, 1951.

SECTION 1

Reading Schemes
for Older Backward Pupils

This section includes reading schemes written especially for pupils of approximately nine years and over and includes series for both the pupil who has not made an effective start in learning to read and the pupil who is finding it hard to progress beyond the early stages. The interest appeal of the books listed is mature and no series is included that has not been written with the needs of the older backward child in view.

THE CHALLENGE READERS C. Niven (Holmes McDougall)

BOYS AND GIRLS	pp.	RA	IA	Price
Book A: Jack and Betty	32	5—6	8- 12	24p
Book B: On the Farm		6—7		
Book C: Holiday Time				
Book D: Rescue at Sea		7—8		
Book E: The Fancy Dress Party				
Book F: The Missing Professor		8—9		
Book G: The Secret of the Cave				
Book H: Christmas in Canada				

Covers   Printed, coloured linson.

Printing   Fair. Type graded 24pt. to 10pt. Pages frequently have an uneven appearance due to changes in the line spacing.

Illustrations   One on almost every page, printed in three-colour process.

Vocabulary   Restricted and graded, but difficulty level and vocabulary load rise rather steeply.

Appraisal   In designing these books for very retarded readers in the top grades of primary schools, the author has recognized the need of such children for interesting and exciting stories combined with solid training in phonic skills. But by attempting to cover too much ground in comparatively few pages, he does not really achieve his object. The stories are fresh and have some interesting features but they are too slight to allow sufficient practice in consolidating the vocabulary covered and in exercising the phonic skills taught in the drills.
As they stand, these books will be useful as supplements to other series, and for providing individual work assignments that can be completed with little supervision by even very poor readers.

ADVENTURES IN READING G. Keir (Oxford University Press)

BOYS AND GIRLS	pp.	RA	IA	Price
Section 1				
6 Adventures in Reading	16	5—7	8—12	12p
5 Supplementary Adventures in Reading				12p
6 Adventures in Writing				12p
Crossword Puzzle Book No. 2				8p
Section 2				
6 More Adventures in Reading	16	7—8	8—14	12p
5 Supplementary More Adventures in Reading				12p
6 More Adventures in Writing				12p
Section 3				
6 New Adventures in Reading	32	8—9	8- 14	15p
6 New Adventures in Writing				13p
Crossword Puzzle Book No. 1				11p
Teacher's Companion				60p

Covers   Sections 1 and 2: Thin card; stapled covers of poor durability, Section 3: Readers, imitation cloth.

Printing   Good. Section 1 and 2: 18pt. type; Section 3: 14 pt. type.

Illustrations Very attractive coloured sketches on almost every page.

Vocabulary Controlled in early books and restricted in others. Short simple sentence construction.

Appraisal These books have a perennial appeal to slow-learning children. They are cheap yet attractive and, being small, can be read at one sitting, giving the slower pupil the pleasure of completing a good story. The subjects include such diverse themes as Red Indians, camping, the circus and mysterious robberies. 'Adventures in Writing' are workbooks, page references throughout indicating the parallel 'Adventure in Reading'. Various exercises help to consolidate sight vocabulary and teach other reading skills. However, they tend to overwork rather limited material, with the result that some pupils find them a little boring. The 'Crossword Puzzle Books' provide an unusual way of checking understanding and mastery of vocabulary.

Titles include:
  Section 1: A Holiday on the Farm   Guy Fawkes Day
  Section 2: Tracking Adventures   Adventures in the Snow
  Section 3: Crooked Cargo   The Lodger in Ludgate Lane

COWBOY SAM BOOKS

Edna Walker Chandler
(E. J. Arnold)

BOYS	pp.	RA	IA	Price
Cowboy Sam and Dandy				33p
Cowboy Sam and Big Bill	48	5–6	8–14	33p
Cowboy Sam and Miss Lily	64	5½–6½	8–14	38p
Cowboy Sam				
Cowboy Sam and Flop	64	6–7	8–14	38p
Cowboy Sam and Freddy				
Cowboy Sam and Freckles				38p
Cowboy Sam and Porky				
Cowboy Sam and Shorty				

Covers Paper covered boards with cased backs.

Printing Excellent; clear type graded 24pt. to 14 pt. Easy to read, attractively laid out pages.

Illustrations Vivid action sketches printed in three colour litho, which should appeal to most boys. One on every page.

Vocabulary Controlled. The vocabulary load, which ranges from 65 different words in the first book to 245 in the last, is light enough to be coped with by the slowest reader. The choice of words is such that most of them would be immediately useful to children in other reading situations.

Appraisal Films and television have made cowboys from the American West as commonplace as our next-door neighbour, but they retain their inimitable appeal. These books make use of this attraction to motivate older backward children who have shown little interest in other reading.
These books should appeal to every boy, and quite a lot of girls as well. Cowboy Sam is tough, practical and ingenious, yet he is gentle and very much one of the 'goodies'. He and the other characters, such as his nephew Freddie, Bill, the

29

cook and the various ranch hands and horses come alive within the pages of the books. The stories include adventures with horses and ranch pets, and being a twentieth-century cowboy, Sam uses modern equipment such as jeeps and bulldozers.

The books are carefully graded and are particularly well suited to the needs of older boys, either for class work or as supplementary readers.

OXFORD COLOUR READING BOOKS and OXFORD JUNIOR WORKBOOKS C. Carver and C. H. Stowasser (Oxford University Press)

Boys and Girls	pp.	RA	IA	Price
Readers				
Grade 1: Red, six titles	32	6—7	8—14	22p
Grade 2: Yellow, six titles				22p
Grade 3: Blue, six titles	32	6½—7½	8—14	22p
Grade 4: Green, six titles				22p
Grade 5: Purple, three titles	32	7—8	8—14	22p
Grade 6: Grey, two titles	48			30p
Workbooks				
Book 1	48	5—6	7—12	20p
Book 2		5½—6½		
Book 3		6—7		
Book 4		6—7		

Covers Readers: Printed, illustrated linen-faced card. Workbooks: Stiff paper.

Printing Good. Very clear 18pt. type with original and attractive page layout. The workbooks are clearly laid out, using several type faces.

Illustrations More pictures than words. The illustration are most amusing and are beautifully reproduced by three-colour litho.

Vocabulary Very severely restricted and controlled, using colour names as key words. The reason for the choice of the particular vocabulary of the readers is not clear, but sometimes the words seem a little unusual for the type of child likely to be using books at this level.

Appraisal *Readers:* The first impression one receives on looking through these books is that they are exceptionally attractive and have what appears to be a challenging and original approach to the problem of children making very slow progress towards literacy. As well as being amusing and decorative, the books include a variety of exercises designed to consolidate the learning of sight vocabulary and to test comprehension, and their particular manner of presentation gains the interest of children who show little regard for more conventionally designed material.

On second reading, one becomes a little doubtful about whether the books are really as good as one first thought. It is little use relying on gaining a child's interest, if this is not leading to further learning, and in the first twenty-four books of this series, surprisingly little ground is covered. The more recent titles, in Grades 5 and 6, are slightly more solid, but even at these higher levels there are no more than a few simple sentences per page and word recognition is still being taught solely on a look-and-say basis.

Workbooks: There is nothing in these workbooks or in the publisher's notes that associates them with the readers, but they are by the same authors and use similar vocabulary with colour names as key words. To this author, they seem to complement each other, the workbooks providing the introduction to phonics and structural analysis that is conspicuously missing from the readers. But, as with the readers, the plan behind the workbooks is hard to discover, the introductory notes giving only the briefest clues to the authors' intentions. These attractive books are badly in need of an explanation from the authors as to the philosophy on which they are based and also the way in which they are intended to be used.

Titles include:

Red: Fun Time	*Yellow:* The Chimp	*Blue:* The Bird Watchers
Green: The Crocodile	*Purple:* Stumpy	*Grey:* The Mist

TEMPO BOOKS   P. Groves and L. Stratta   (Longmans, Green)

Boys and Girls	pp.	RA	IA	Price
Book 1: The Swinging Kings	45	6–7	10–14	40p
Book 2: The Big Drop	47	6½–7½		
Book 3: Lost in the Fog		7–8		
Book 4: The Club Dance		7–8		
Book 5: Sandra Helps the Gang		7½–8½		
Book 6: At The Market		7½–8½		
Book 7: Bonfire Night		8–9		
Book 8: The Trap		8–9		
Book 9: The Fair		8–9		
Book 10: At the Circus		8–9		

Covers   Subtly coloured card with a gay appearance and arresting illustrations.

Printing   Excellent; type graded 18pt. to 14pt. Well laid out pages with wide margins and well placed illustrations.

Illustrations   One on every page, either in full colour litho or in black and white.

Vocabulary   Very carefully controlled on a phonic basis with the number of sight words introduced coming mainly from the hundred most frequently used words in the English language. Both phonic and sight word lists are included.

Appraisal   Being both attractive and amusing, these books should interest many older children with severe reading problems but the shortness of the incidents in the earlier books and the lack of originality in the stories may make them less popular than might be expected.

Although designed as a complete reading scheme, no exercises are included to test either comprehension or word recognition skills.

The books' main purpose is likely to be as supplementary readers for youngsters making very slow progress.

PATHFINDER BOOKS   J. and P. Bradley   (Oliver and Boyd)

Boys	pp.	RA	IA	Price
Graded Readers				
Book 1	128	7–8	9–16	25p
Book 3: Trouble in the Air		8–9		25p
Book 5: Trouble in Store		9–10		25p

Covers Book 1: durable linson; Books 3 and 5: paper-covered boards of only fair durability.

Printing Good; clear and well-arranged pages with type graded 18pt. to 12pt.

Illustrations Two-colour litho; plentiful and amusing.

Vocabulary 445 words used in the first reader. Vocabulary lists in each graded reader. Graded sentence length and paragraph structure.

Appraisal Although it may be regarded as the hardy perennial of remedial teaching, this series remains particularly useful with older backward boys. Its major theme is the activities of a group of lads training to be sailors, airmen and dockworkers. Each chapter is followed by valuable word-building and comprehension exercises. In Book 5, there is a change of format, all the exercises being assembled in a single section at the end of the book. This improvement enables the reader to enjoy the story (a really good yarn about small-boat sailing) without the constant distraction of the text being interspersed with exercises. Unfortunately, much of this series is now out of print, but what remains available is still useful and worthwhile.

RESCUE READING SERIES   James Webster   (Ginn)

Boys and Girls	pp.	RA	IA	Price
Rescue Stories				
Shorty the Hero	64	6–7	7–12	30p
Shorty and The Rabbit	48			
Shorty and the Bank Robbers	48	6½–7½	7–12	30p
Sally the Seagull				
Martin the Mouse	64	7–8	7–12	30p
Brown Beauty				
More Rescue Stories				
Patrick the Parrot	64	8–9	8–14	30p
Hoppy the Second				
Snowball				
Shorty Again				
Firewater				
Trouble the Fox				
Workbooks				
Finding Words	32	6–7	7–9	13p
Code Words	32	6½–7½		
Puzzle Words	32	7–8		
Cut-and Stick Book 1	28	6–7	7–9	14p
Cut-and-Stick Book 2	28	6½–7½	7–9	14p
Teacher's Book—Reading Failure	32			30p
Programme Pads				
For Shorty the Hero				11p
For Shorty and the Rabbit				14p
For Shorty and the Bank Robbers				14p

Covers   Story Books: beautifully illustrated coloured linson stitched backs. Workbooks and Cut-and-Stick Books: coloured paper.

Printing   Excellent. Rescue and More Rescue Stories: 24pt. bold-faced serif type with all direct speech printed in red; well laid-out but the choice of type face seems overly large for the age-group for whom this series is apparently intended. Workbooks: mainly 24pt. sans-serif type printed in two colours with some exercise details in 14pt. type.

Illustrations   Sensitive, colourful water-colours, superbly reproduced in four colour litho. The animal studies, in particular, are delightful, avoiding both sentimentality and anthropomorphism.

Vocabulary   Carefully controlled and graded. Very simple sentence structure throughout. Practice in difficult and unfamiliar words is given by the Cut-and-Stick Books, and phonic analysis and word-building are dealt with in the Workbooks.

Appraisal   The 'Rescue Reading Series' is one of the most visually attractive series published recently. Intended for poor readers in the upper junior school, it will also be extremely useful in ESN classes. The stories are simple, each one dealing with a situation in which a well-beloved pet does some service for its master. They are happy, exciting stories with no artificially induced emotionality. They are carefully graded and the vocabulary is simple but such as children between 7 and 12 years would use in every day speech.
The expendable workbooks, although attractively produced, are less useful. The amount of actual work the pupil has to do on each page is severely limited and the purpose of some of the exercises is obscure. The Teacher's Book describes the author's views on remedial teaching and offers many suggestions on activities and organisation of the reading programme.

TREND   Eds. B. Bird, A. Scanlon & J. A. Hart   (Ginn)

Boys and Girls	pp.	RA	IA	Price
The Dark House	60	6½–7½	10–14	30p
Watcher on the Wharf				
Robbie				
Some Trannie That	68	7–8	10–14	30p
Old Bootleg				
A Real Hero				
Coffee at Charlies	80	7½–8½	10–16	30p
Bindi-Eye	88			
Crash Landing	98			
A Fabulous Day in the Life of				
Professor Mugwump	88	8–9	10–16	3op
Gaye Lizzie	74			
Cry on a Foggy Night	98	8½–9½	10–16	30p
Snow at Tataru				

Further titles and workbooks are in preparation.

Covers   Fully-coloured, illustrated laminated card; paperback size and format.

Printing   Excellent; 14pt. serif type carefully arranged in short units. Two titles— 'Some Trannie That' and 'Coffee at Charlies' were the 1970 winners of the Transfield Award for Book Design in Australia.

Illustrations   Basically black and white drawings with an extra colour on some pages. A variety of styles has been used, with varying degrees of success. Illustrations are frequent and most effective when they occupy a full page.

Vocabulary   Very carefully restricted and graded, with the basic vocabulary chosen from the Dolch lists of most frequently used words. As far as possible the linguistic patterns and vocabulary of the secondary school child have been used in the stories.

Appraisal   These books, which originated in Australia, are a serious attempt to provide contemporary idiomatic reading material for a specific group of pupils, namely reluctant or backward teenagers in technical and secondary schools. The authors have had considerable experience teaching in Victorian high schools and draft versions of the books were tried on their pupils and altered in the light of these trials before publication. The language and the themes are of today's youth and thus they may date more quickly than traditional books, but their inexpensiveness makes this a minor problem. The rather racy language may not appeal to all teachers and students, but for others the idiom will be sufficiently appealing to entice reluctant readers to the printed page.

NEW READING   Ed. A. F. Scott   (Reader's Digest, U.K.)

Boys and Girls	pp.	RA	IA	Price
Blue Series				
Junior Book 1	118	7—7½	8—12	20p
Junior Book 2	118	7½—8	8—12	
Book 1	118	8—8½	8—12	
Book 2	118	8½—9	8—12	
Book 3	118	9—10	9—14	
Book 4	118	10—11	10—16	
Book 5	118	11—12	10—16	
Red Series		parallel to above		
New Reading Answer Book				25p

Covers   Attractively printed linson; stitched backs.

Printing   Good; mainly 12pt. type but other sizes and contrasting type faces introduced for variety. Clear page layout.

Illustrations   Very pleasant line-and-wash drawings on almost every page. Some full-page plates.

Vocabulary   Although not controlled, some attempt has been made at restriction and grading. Difficult words are printed in a box at the beginning of each extract, for special word study.

Appraisal   These books contain selections and extracts, carefully shortened and simplified, from articles originally published in 'Reader's Digest'. They are topical, interesting and well out of the rut of the usual passages chosen for English study. Each extract is followed by exercises on comprehension and vocabulary extension. These are well thought out and encourage careful reading and word study, and also give many opportunities for class discussion and suggestions for further reading about the subjects studied.

Articles include:

Flying Doctors of the Outback
Strange Things About Your Dog

The King's Present
Our Friend the Earth Worm

THE SPRINGBOARD BOOKS   C. Niven   (E. J. Arnold)

Boys and Girls	pp.	RA	IA	Price
Book 1: The Fishing Trip	32	7—8	9—14	23p
Book 2: Milton Aerodrome				

Covers   Brightly coloured linson.

Printing   Good. Clear 12pt. type and attractively laid-out pages.

Illustrations   Printed in two-colour litho. Style of drawing is rather unattractive.

Vocabulary   Restricted and graded. Word-building lists based on the text are provided.

Appraisal   This series gives the initial impression of being better than it actually is. Its bright appearance, arresting titles and the wealth of illustrations lead the casual observer to expect that the books will be particularly tempting to the jaded appetites of pupils in the higher primary grades who have minimal reading skills. Unfortunately, closer inspection reveals faults which makes these books, attractive as they are, less valuable than could be wished for. The stories, whilst having exciting possibilities, cannot be developed sufficiently in the sixteen pages allotted to them to give the variety of incident necessary to hold the attention of poorer readers. At the same time, the books do not give sufficient practice in reading the vocabulary introduced and do not provide sufficient material to support sixteen pages of exercises, albeit that these are varied, useful and original. As they stand, these books will be useful for practice in silent reading for comprehension and for homework assignments, but they are not substantial enough to be used as a basis for reading instruction for backward readers unless they are supported by a great deal of other material.

STEP UP AND READ   W. R. Jones   (University of London Press)

Boys	pp.	RA	IA	Price
Book A: Bob Adams and His Family	16	7—8	9—14	13p
Book B: The Car Outing				
Book C: Bob Joins the Club	32	7½—8½	9—14	15p
Book D: 'The Dirty Duck' Grows Wings				
Book E: The Winning Kick	32	8—9	9—14	15p
Companion Exercises 1	48	6—7		20p
Companion Exercises 2	48	7—8		20p
Companion Exercises 3	44	8—9		20p
Phonic Cards				38p per set
Teacher's Book	48			25p

Covers   Story Books: coloured, illustrated card. Companion Exercises plain coloured card. Stitched backs.

Printing   Good; layout clear and easy to follow, particularly in the exercises.

Illustrations   Rather dull black and white drawings.

Vocabulary   Closely related throughout to the sounds taught initially by the Phonic Cards. The first readers use only phonically regular words. The use of irregular words is then gradually increased until Book E uses a normal but simple vocabulary.

Appraisal   Designed as an intensive scheme for use with older boys both in remedial classes and special schools, this series is based on a systematic phonic approach. It aims at making it possible for a comparatively inexperienced teacher to give relatively individualized instruction to a class with a varied range of reading ages and learning capacities. Being carefully planned and attractively produced, the series is excellent in its way, but the simplicity of its stories and their predominantly domestic back-ground makes it unlikely to appeal to the brighter child with specific reading difficulties. This series will be most useful in schools for educationally sub-normal children.

LONGMANS STRUCTURAL READERS   Various authors
(Longmans, Green)

Boys	pp.	RA	IA	Price
Stage 1: 4 titles	16	7–8	10–16	10p
Stage 2: 6 titles	32	7½–8½	10–16	
Stage 3: 7 titles + 7 1-act plays	68	8–9	10–16	20p
Stage 4: 5 titles + 3 plays	90	8½–9½	12-adult	
Stage 5: 4 titles + 2 plays	84	9–10	12-adult	
Stage 6: 4 titles + 3 plays	74	9–10	12-adult	
Handbook	48			

Covers   Illustrated, plastic-coated card; stapled backs.

Printing   Good. Type graded 14pt.–10pt. with exercises in smaller faces. Stages 1 and 2 are arranged in comic strip form; other stages have conventional page layout and the rather small type face chosen makes the pages look overcrowded

Illustrations   Stages 1 and 2: full colour litho with as much illustration as text. Stages 3 and 4: two-colour litho with frequent half-page plates interspersed throughout the text.
Stages 5 and 6: a few black and white full-page plates in each book.

Vocabulary   Very carefully restricted and graded, using a basic vocabulary listed in the Handbook and a few essential interest words. The sentence structure and grammatical complexity is also carefully graded according to a linguistic scheme set out in the Handbook.

Appraisal   This series incorporates many of the latest ideas put forward for teaching English as a foreign language and the careful planning, gentle grading of both vocabulary and structure and the high interest level of the stories make it as useful in remedial work as in its original purpose. The books will be especially valuable as supplementary readers with older boys and with adults with reduced reading skills. The earlier books are mainly original, simple but exciting adventure yarns whilst the later stages include mainly carefully re-written versions of modern novels. Simple comprehension and English usage exercises are included at the end of each book.

Titles include:

Stage 1:
The Prisoners
King Henry
Stage 4:
The Prisoner of Zenda
The Thirty Nine Steps

Stage 2:
On the Road
April Fool's Day
Stage 5:
Kidnapped
The Sign of Indra

Stage 3:
Down the River
Mosquito Town
Stage 6:
Modern Short Stories
The Young Warriors

THE BURGESS BOOKS   C. V. Burgess   (University of London Press)

Boys and Girls	pp.	RA	IA	Price
Readers				
Books 1a, 1b, 1c, 1d	32	7–8	9–14	13p
Books 2a, 2b, 2c, 2d	32	7½–8½		13p
Books 3a, 4a	32	8–9		13p
Workbooks 1a, 1b, 1c, 1d	24	7–8	9–14	9p
Workbooks 2a, 2b, 2c, 2d		7½–8		9p
Workbooks 3a, 4a		8–9		9p
Plays				
Books 1 and 2	32	8–9		10p
Books 3 and 4				

Covers   Readers and Plays: Atractively illustrated coloured linson.
Workbooks: paper.

Printing   Readers: Good; clear 12pt. type; interesting and spacious page layout.
Workbooks: designed to be expendable. Well-planned to give adequate space for
answers.
Plays: Good; 12pt. type; printed in a format which makes them very easy to use
as scripts for play-readings.

Illustrations   Cartoon-like, black and white drawings which are ugly but amusing.

Vocabulary   Slightly restricted and roughly graded in difficulty. Clear vigorous
style but the humour is occasionally a little laboured.

Appraisal   This scheme includes a series of amusing adventure stories written
especially for backward readers who need persuading to use their limited reading
skills. These tales are credible yet packed with action.
The workbooks aim at improving comprehension of what is read and consolidating learning through activity. Sometimes the exercises seem lacking in purpose.
The books of playlets are particularly useful. Each book contains four short plays,
often introducing the same characters and backgrounds as the stories. They are
full of simple, direct characterization and are well within the capacity of most
backward readers.

Titles include:

Stories: The Soap Box Derby   The Inventor's Club
Plays: The Lost Pipe   The Gift Bomb

DATA P. Young (Schofield and Sims)

Boys	pp.	RA	IA	Price
Stage 1				
Data 1: Told by an Arrow	32	8—9	10—14	25p
Data 2: Zig and Zag from Planet ZV 7	58			40p
Data 3: The First Workbook	32			13p
Stage 2:				
Data 4: Rik and Kara	56	8½—9½	10—14	30p
Data 5: Zig the Great and Zag the Big	72			40p
Data 6: The Second Workbook	32			13p
Stage 3:				
Data 7: A Dog for Jerry	76	8½—9½	10—14	30p
Data 8: Trouble with Bruff	88			30p
Data 9: The Third Workbook	32			13p
Stage 4:				
Data 10: Data on Cowboys	78	9—10	10—14	45p
Data 11: Dead Man's Trail	88			30p
Data 12: The Fourth Workbook	32			13p
Stage 5				
Data 13: The Data Book of 'Joe Miller' Jokes	56	9—10	10—14	30p
Data 14: Once Upon a Space	102			35p
Data 15: The Fifth Workbook	32			13p

Covers   Coloured and illustrated coated card or linson for the reading books; coloured paper for the workbooks. The books are in a variety of sizes and bindings.

Printing   Good. There is a wide variety of type faces and styles of layout and, on the whole, a high standard of printing and appearance.

Illustrations   Again, there is a wide variety of styles, some being in full colour, others in two-colour litho, monochrome or black-and-white. The overall effect is lively and animating.

Vocabulary   Restricted and slightly graded with sentence and paragraph structure kept simple throughout.

Appraisal   Apparently designed for use with slower learning children in the lower classes of secondary schools, this is a cheerful and varied collection of books which will provide a useful basis for a practical and stimulating English course. The stories are original, interesting and geared to the tastes of the children who will read them, yet at the same time introduce a wealth of useful factual material.
The expendable workbooks are well thought out and include many useful exercises aimed at both increasing vocabulary and reading skills and at improving written English.

THE BOOSTER BOOKS   W. C. H. Chalk   (Heinemann)

Boys	pp.	RA	IA	Price
Level 1				
The Man from Mars	128	8–9	9–14	38p
Old Ugly				38p
Workbooks 1 and 2	32			13p
Level 2				
The Secret Factory	128	8½–9½	9–14	38p
The Talking Machine				38p
Workbook 3	32			13p
Level 3				
The Gomez Story	128	9–10	9–16	38p
H.M.S. Thing				38p
Workbook 4	32			13p
Level 4				
Escape from Bondage	128	9–10	9–16	38p
The Spider Bomb				38p
Level 5				
Mask of Dusk	128	9½–10½	12–18	38p
The Gnomids				
Workbook 5	32			13p

Covers   Readers: illustrated, cloth-covered boards. Workbooks: coloured paper.

Printing   Good. Readers: 12pt. type; well spaced, conventional page layout. Workbooks: 12pt. serif and italic type; well-planned pages making optimum use of available space to include a variety of different exercises, but avoiding an over-crowded appearance.

Illustrations   Readers: occasional amusing black and white line drawings. Workbooks: nil.

Vocabulary   Restricted and graded with very simple sentence structure and short paragraphs. The workbooks provide a systematic revision of the commoner phonic and structural units.

Appraisal   Like most teachers who specialize in this field, the author of this series, who is responsible for the teaching of slow-learners in a secondary modern school realizes that two of the major educational needs of such children are a desire to read and an ability to tackle new words. To satisfy such needs there must be a supply of interesting yet simple books and some means of systematic and meaningful training in reading skills. This series succeeds to some extent in catering for both. The readers are fast-moving, exciting stories with a strong element of science fiction, which few pupils, however blasé about school, will fail to enjoy.

The workbooks are thoughtfully planned and cover the most commonly used phonic units and simple syllables. Meaningfulness is stressed throughout and the exercises, although requiring effort on the part of the pupil, are yet not so difficult as to be discouraging. However, unfortunately these books are dull, both to look at and to work from. A few illustrations and, perhaps, a few short stories to break the monotony of the stream of exercises would be an improvement.

Supplementary Reading Material for Older Pupils

This section includes both graded series and sets of books written at or about a particular level of reading difficulty. Each series chosen will appeal to children older in years than the level of reading indicates. Such books provide the basis for class libraries in special schools and are sources of ancillary reading materials in remedial work. They have been chosen mainly for their entertainment value, are mostly quite short, and, in the main, comparatively inexpensive, so that it should be possible to have a fair selection of them. It is hoped that by offering reluctant readers a wide variety of good stories at an appropriate difficulty level, they will be encouraged and stimulated, and eventually develop the invaluable habit of reading for pleasure. Also, through this extra practice in palatable form, the skills learnt in more formal teaching will be consolidated.

THE LOOKOUT GANG M. B. Chapman (Robert Gibson)

BOYS AND GIRLS	pp.	RA	IA	Price
Book 1: The Gang Meets	32	5—6	8—12	21p
Book 2: The Gang and the Pay Grab		5½—6½		
Book 3: The Gang and the Mail Train Robbers		6—7		
Book 4: The Gang and the Stolen Bicycle		6½—7½		
Book 5: The Gang and the Smuggler		7—8		
Book 6: The Gang and the Airport Car Thieves		7½—8½		

Covers   Printed, linen-faced card; stapled backs.

Printing   Good; type graded 24pt. to 18pt. sans-serif type. Carefully planned spacious layout, but the arrangement of the lines does not take careful enough account of the necessity to make the breaks in the sentences at appropriate places to encourage continuity of thought.

Illustrations   Well-drawn black-and-white pictures with plenty of action. Half-page plates on almost every page.

Vocabulary   Carefully controlled with a strong phonic bias. The grading of difficulty is rather steep. Word lists are provided at the end of each book.

Appraisal   This simple but carefully graded and constructed series would be a useful set of books to be used with children being taught by a predominantly phonic method using a teaching kit without associated books such as D. H. Stott's Programmed Reading Kit.[1] The stories are mainly about the detective activities of a group of boys and girls, and are both exciting yet believable. They are better reading than most stories written at such a low reading level.

SEA HAWK BOOKS Sheila K. McCullagh, MA (E. J. Arnold)

BOYS	pp.	RA	IA	Price
Introductory Books				
Book 1: The Rescue	16	6—7	9—12	18p
Book 2: The Lighthouse				
Main Readers				
Book 1: The Sea Hawk	32	6½—7½	9—12	28p
Book 2: The Shipwreck				
Book 3: Smuggler's Island				
Book 4: The Smuggler's Knife				
Library Books				
Book 1: The Vikings	32	7—8	9—12	33p
Book 2: King Halfdan's Sons				
Book 3: The Dragon of the Sea				
Book 4: Mutiny at Sea				

Covers   Introductory Books: printed, illustrated linson.
Main Readers: illustrated, paper-covered boards.
Library Books: paper-covered boards with illustrated dust covers.

---

[1] D. H. Stott. *Programmed Reading Kit.* Edinburgh, Holmes, McDougall Ltd.

Printing   Excellent. Introductory Books: clear 24pt. serif type, well arranged in short sentences.
Main Readers: 14pt. serif type, double-spaced and arranged in easy-to-read units.
Library Books: conventionally spaced 14pt. type.

Illustrations   Delicate, rather idealized pictures, mainly in two-colour litho, but some exquisitely reproduced in full colour. Half-page plate on every page.

Vocabulary   Controlled and graded

Appraisal   Although these books are exceptionally beautiful to look at, and, at first glance, their themes and stories seem suitable for older boys with reading problems, inspection suggests that they will be unacceptable to any boy aware of the toughness and brutality of real life. To youngsters over twelve years old, the artificiality which pervades these books is likely to prove offensive. The harshness of sea-faring life at the time of sailing vessels and smugglers has been glamorized and toned down too much. Even murder is dealt with discreetly, without emotion. Life at sea, one feels, was never like this!
This is a pity, for with a little more toughness, a sturdier realism, these books could have been acceptable to a wide range of readers. They will, however, be useful additions to class libraries in upper primary schools, providing light reading for both the advanced younger child and the slower older one.

ADVENTURES IN SPACE   S. McCullagh   (Rupert Hart-Davis)

BOYS	pp.	RA	IA	Price
Moon-flight. Books 1, 2, & 3				20p
Journey to Mars, Books 1, 2, & 3	32	7–8	10–14	
Red Planet, Books 1, 2, & 3				
Journey to a New Earth				

Covers   Illustrated and coloured linson; stapled backs.

Printing   Excellent. 14pt. sans-serif type. Elegant, unconventional page layout combining text and illustrations into an attractive whole which is very easy to read.

Illustrations   Stylised, monochrome drawings which reflect the strangeness of outer space and the general science fiction background of the series.

Vocabulary   That of the 'Journey to Mars' books is restricted with the emphasis on common, phonetically regular monosyllabic words. There is a salting of harder words added to maintain the interest level.

Appraisal   Designed to interest older boys with limited reading skills, this series provides science fiction of the type popularized by 'Dan Dare'. The books have an atmosphere of suspense, danger and courage against abnormal odds. Most boys will enjoy them as supplementary readers.

THE GO READERS   M. Calman   (Blond Educational)

BOYS AND GIRLS	pp.	RA	IA	Price
Books 1–4	32	7–8	10–16	20p

Covers   Shiny, paper-covered boards.

Printing   Good. 12pt. type. Pages arranged with words in short lines on one side of the page only.

Illustrations   Black and white sketches on every other page. These bold, realistic drawings reflect the modern 'teen-age' atmosphere of the stories.

Vocabulary   Severely restricted: racy without being slangy or ungrammatical.

Appraisal   Martin Calman is a newcomer to the ranks of those who write specifically for poor readers, but he appears to be a man who not only likes young people, but recognizes that self-reliance and good sense can exist together with long hair, leather jackets and a liking for the 'top twenty'. His attitude is reflected in these simple but warm and lively stories with their backgrounds of coffee bars, youth clubs and city streets and their themes of shortage of money, sudden domestic crises and conflict of loyalties between home and peer group. There is no artificial glamour about these books, but instead a fresh, direct approach which should have an immediate appeal to semi-literate pupils in secondary schools.

Titles

What About Fred?	Can Red Ride?
Ron's First Round	Ted Makes a Splash

FAR AND NEAR READERS   Various authors   (Chambers)

BOYS AND GIRLS	pp.	RA	IA	Price
First series				
Red Books 1—4 (R2-O.P.)	24	7—8	9—12	10p
Blue Books B5 only	32	8—9	9—14	
Green Books G3 only	32	9—10		
Second Series				
Yellow Books 1—4	32	7—8	9—12	10p
Orange Books 1—3		8—9	9—14	
Mauve Books M6 and M7 only		9—10		

Covers   Coloured linson; stitched backs

Printing   Good; type graded 18pt. to 12pt.

Illustrations   Frequent lively black and white sketches.

Vocabulary   Restricted and graded, with a few rather harder words introduced to make interesting stories possible. These are listed in the teacher's book. Short, direct sentences.

Appraisal   This is an excellent supplementary series for older children which has the additional advantage of several titles written especially for girls, including one with a Canadian background with the intriguing title of 'Where is Cousin Angus?' The stories have a wide variety of settings including Gibraltar, California and an Australian sheep station. Many of these books could be used in conjunction with social studies lessons.

Titles include:

The Real Team Spirit   Greasepaint and Footlights   That Boy Joe

TEENAGE TWELVE   Richardson, Whitehouse & Wilkinson   (Robert Gibson)

BOYS AND GIRLS	pp.	RA	IA	Price
Book 1: Youth Club	16	7–8	12–16	16p
Book 2: Beach Days				
Book 3: Fun Fair				
Book 4: Firefighters	16	7½–8½	12–16	16p
Book 5: Man on the Beat				
Book 6: A New Games Shed				
Book 7: Sports Day	16	8–9	12–16	16p
Book 8: At The Farm				
Book 9: Away Match				
Book 10: Day Trippers				
Book 11: Behind the Scenes				
Book 12: In the Nick of Time				

Covers   Printed and illustrated linen-faced paper; stapled backs.

Printing   Fair; type graded from 14 to 12 pt. sans-serif type with the particular phonic sound being practised in each section printed in bold type. Some of the books have an over-crowded appearance, due to a rather cramped layout.

Illustrations   Detailed and rather fussy pictures, printed in black and white or two-colour litho. At least one on every page.

Vocabulary   This is based on the Dolch basic list of 220 words with some additional, and frequently rather difficult words added for interest. At the same time there is a strong phonic bias, the commoner sounds in English being worked through systematically. Word lists are given at the end of each book.

Appraisal   Aimed at the really poor reader in the secondary school, these little books provide attractive tales that deal with the interests of such pupils—Youth clubs, Coffee Bars and T.V. at a simple level which will appeal particularly to slow-learning children. The stories are short and each section is followed by comprehension exercises. Too slight to be used as a complete reading scheme, these little books will be excellent for providing individual assignments for silent reading and homework.

THE INNER RING BOOKS   A. Pullen, C. Rapstoff & M. Hardcastle   (Ernest Benn)

BOYS AND GIRLS	pp.	RA	IA	Price
First Series				
Twelve titles	32	7–8	12–16	25p limp
				40p library
Second Series				
Twelve titles	32	7–8	12–16	

Covers   Paper-covered boards, with brightly coloured, illustrated jackets on glossy paper.

Printing   Excellent. 18pt. sans-serif type; attractive and well-arranged page layout.

Illustrations   Dashing black-and-white sketches aimed at arousing the immediate interest of the non-academic child.

Vocabulary   Carefully restricted and managing, without using slang of unacceptable usage, to reflect the idiom of the teenager. Very simple sentence construction.

Appraisal   Designed to obtain the interest of that section of the school population that considers the classroom as a resting place between home and the coffee-bar, these attractive books reflect the sub-culture from which so many poor readers come. The stories are down-to-earth, racy and exciting. They accept realistically the restrictions and limitations of such an environment, yet lay emphasis throughout on the positive qualities of family life and of law and order. Unfortunately the choice of the present tense in many of the stories gives them a slightly artificial air which may be unacceptable to some pupils. The recently added second series is slightly more sophisticated in its approach, and will attract those youngsters who have begun to appreciate a good story and who are also becoming aware of some of the social problems in the world around them.

Titles include:
First Series:
On the Hook	A Night in Town
The Last Straw	Fox Fair

Second Series
Dive to Danger	Reds & Blues
Stop that Car	Strike

CHALLENGE BOOKS   A. E. Smith   (Holmes, McDougall)

BOYS AND GIRLS	pp.	RA	IA	Price
Books 1—15	32	7—8	8—15	19p
Books 15—21		8—9		
Books 22—27		7—8		

Covers   Brightly coloured linson with stitched backs

Printing   Good; 14pt. type. Well spaced layout, very suitable for children with limited reading ability.

Illustrations   Line and wash; an illustration at the top or bottom of every page.

Vocabulary   Restricted; careful but unstilted repetition.

Appraisal   These excellent adventure stories are most successful in their appeal to very backward older readers. Their style is fresh and vigorous, their plots are original, and they have proved themselves to be first-rate supplementary material.

Titles include:
The Garage Gang	One Dark Night
The Runaway	Susie Swims

THE WORLD'S GREAT STORIES   Ed. M. Dingle   (Oxford University Press)

BOYS AND GIRLS	pp.	RA	IA	Price
Three titles	80	7½—8½	10—14	20p

Covers   Stiff, printed card.

Printing   Good; clear 14pt. type; very little text on each page.

Illustrations   Black and white drawings on each page.

Vocabulary   Severely restricted; very simple sentence construction.

Appraisal   Intended originally for deaf children, these very simple versions of well-known stories will be invaluable for use with severely retarded readers. The stories chosen will appeal to many older children whose inadequate reading skills deny them the experience of reading the original books.

THE ASHLEY BOOKS   B. Ashley   (Mills & Boon with Allman)

BOYS	pp.	RA	IA	Price
Four titles				
Junior versions	90	7½—8½	10—14	23p & 15p
Senior versions	128	9—10		28p & 20p

Covers   Printed card or paper-covered boards.

Printing   Good; 12pt. type; conventional page layout.

Vocabulary   Severely restricted with very simple sentence structure in the Junior versions; restricted and simplified in the Senior versions.

Appraisal   These books of short stories, written at two levels of difficulty, aim at providing good yarns for slower readers in secondary schools. Unfortunately, the stories have little that is original in them, the writing is fragmentary, and, in the Junior versions, the action jumps from place to place so rapidly that it becomes difficult to follow the plots. In spite of this, many children seem to enjoy them as leisure reading.

Titles include: Don't Run Away   Space Shot

SIMON AND DOROTHY STORIES   P. Emmens   (Blond Educational)

GIRLS	pp.	RA	IA	Price
Four titles	72	8—9	10—14	25p

Covers   Coloured, printed linson; cased backs.

Printing   Good; 12pt. type; conventional page layout.

Illustrations   Six full-page black and white sketches in each book.

Vocabulary   Restricted. Simple sentence and paragraph structure.

Appraisal   By treating the love-hate relationship between young adolescent boys and girls with sensitivity and without sentimentality, the author of these books has produced four charming tales. They have a country background, but both themes and situations have an international appeal. These books will be particularly popular with girls in slower streams in secondary schools.

Titles include: Simon to the Rescue   The Man Who Came Back

TRUE ADVENTURE SERIES Jerome, Joyce and Charles (Blackie)

BOYS AND GIRLS	**pp.**	**RA**	**IA**	**Price**
Forty-three titles	28	8–9	10–14	17p

Covers Attractively printed linson with some titles in bright colours.

Printing Excellent; clear 12pt. type. Well-spaced page layout.

Illustrations Two-colour litho; two full-page plates and several smaller ones in each book.

Vocabulary Carefully restricted. Sentences are short and there is much direct speech.

Appraisal This excellent set of modern true adventure stories is planned for the older backward reader who takes little interest in fiction. It contains stories of perpetual interest such as the Flying Doctor Service in Australia, the All-England Tennis Tournament and the ascent of Mount Everest, with new titles being constantly added. The subject matter will increase the reader's knowledge of the world he lives in and provide plenty of points for class discussion and further reading about topical events. However, the teacher should be on the alert, as occasionally the authors' facts are a little inaccurate in detail. Each book contains three stories.
This series is highly recommended.

Titles include:

Tales of the Air	Tales of Rescue
Tales of Brave Girls	Tales of Headhunters

COMPASS READERS A. Burnham (Wheaton)

BOYS	**pp.**	**RA**	**IA**	**Price**
Books 1–5	32	8–9	10–16	15p

Covers Illustrated, printed linson.

Printing Fair; conventional page layout.

Illustrations Simple black and white sketches

Vocabulary Severely restricted. Straightforward style with very simple sentence structure and much direct speech.

Appraisal Stories of war and heroic deeds, both past and present, are guaranteed to find an audience among most adolescent boys. These unpretentious books provide such material at a difficulty level commensurate with the reading abilities of very retarded pupils in the upper classes of ESN schools and in slow-learner's groups within ordinary schools. Each book contains two stories, in three short chapters.

Stories include:

The Wind and the Sea	Blood River
Escape from the Boers	The Lucky Pilot

Introductory Reading Schemes
Suitable for Younger Retarded Readers

This section lists material that has been found particularly useful in remedial work with children from seven to nine years, who have failed to make an effective start in learning to read. It does not pretend to be a comprehensive list of the available infant reading schemes nor does it include those using special methods such as ITA or 'Words in Colour'. Rather, it includes such series as have been shown to be acceptable to a comparatively wide age range. It also includes those few series written especially for children commencing to learn to read from seven years onwards. Some language development schemes have also been included. There is some overlap with Section 1, some of the books recommended there being equally suitable for younger children while many of the books in this section could be used profitably with immature older retarded children, particularly those in ESN schools.

THE FOUNTAIN PICTURE BOOKS   J. Brandon & D. Norris   (Ginn)

BOYS AND GIRLS	pp.	Price
Books 1, 2, 3	32	23p

Covers   Illustrated card.

Printing   Good. Suggestions for stories etc. placed at the bottom of the page so as not to distract from the pictures.

Illustrations   Drawings of familiar objects, people and situations, gradually increasing in complexity. Reproduced in three-colour litho.

Appraisal   Devised in a training centre for moderately and severely mentally retarded children, these picture books provide a graded programme of language stimulation which would be invaluable for use in kindergarten and nursery classes with children who are slower than most in learning language skills and in responding to pre-reading programmes. Text is provided as guidance for parents and teachers.

HAPPY VENTURE READING SCHEME   F. J. Schonell, I. Serjeant and
P. Flowerdew   (Oliver & Boyd)

BOYS AND GIRLS	pp.	RA	IA	Price
Pre-reader: Reading Fun	32	—	5—6	15p
Introductory Book: Fluff and Nip	24	5—6	5—7	15p
Approach Book	16			13p
Playbook: Hide and Seek	24			16p
Library Books 1—5	16			25p per set
Workbook	32			13p
Book 1: Playtime	42	5½—6½	5—7	20p
Playbook: Story Time	48			20p
Library Books 6—10	18			25p per set
Workbook	32			13p
Book 2: Our Friends	48	6—7	5—8	20p
Playbook: Saturday Play	64			20p
Library Books 11—15	18			30p per set
Workbook	32			13p
Book 3: Growing Up	92	6½—7½	5—8	25p
Playbook: Some Stories	92			25p
Library Books 16—21	18			35p per set
Workbook	32			13p
Book 4: Holiday Time	124	7—8	5—9	28p
Playbook: Far and Wide	124			28p
Library Books 22—27	18			40p per set
Workbook	32			13p
Happy Venture Teacher's Manual				
(New Edition)	122			88p

Covers   Readers and Playbooks: soft durable linen. Library books: stiff coloured paper. Each reading level is identified by the colour of its covers.

Printing   Good; clear, graded type 24pt. to 12pt. Page layout carefully planned to encourage good eye-movements.

Illustrations   Those in the readers are in full colour and a lively style. The Playbooks and Library Books are illustrated in two-colour litho and the Workbooks have many line drawings.

Vocabulary   Very strictly controlled (forty-three new words in Introductory Book; sixty-two new words in Book 1. Vocabulary load increases gradually at each level.) All new words are introduced carefully in context, using two or three to a page. The Library Books have the same vocabulary as the readers; the Playbooks add a few new words at each level.

Appraisal   This reading series remains one of the most technically perfect available and its recent revision has increased its value. The stories in the early stages are based on the experiences and immediate environment of the young child. There is a gradual widening of interest in the later books.
Apart from its value in infant's schools, this scheme is helpful in ESN schools and with groups of immature children who are late in learning to read. The wealth of ancillary material ensures complete consolidation of learning at each stage. This material includes introductory cards, matching and comprehension cards, wall strips and pictures, film strips, sets of cellograph pictures and a song book. The Workbooks are particularly valuable, being carefully designed to provide the maximum of purposeful practice and to encourage silent reading for comprehension from the very beginning.
The Teacher's Manual is a helpful guide with an amplitude of suggestions for further work and activities. The theoretical basis of the series is discussed in 'The Psychology and Teaching of Reading' by F. J. Schonell (Published Oliver and Boyd).

McKEE READERS   P. McKee et Al.   (Nelson)

BOYS AND GIRLS	pp.	RA	IA	Price
Getting Ready for Reading	32	–	5–6	30p
Book 1: Tip	48	5–6	5–7	20p
Book 2: Tip and Mitten	48	5½–6½	5–7	20p
Platform Readers A1–6	16	5½–6½	5–7	18p
Book 3: With Peter and Susan	64	6–7	5–8	30p
Platform Readers B1–6	16	6–7	5–8	18p
Book 4: Up and Away	96	6½–7½	5–8	45p
Platform Readers C1–6	16	6½–7½	5–8	18p
Book 5: On we Go	96	7–8	6–9	45p
Platform Readers D1–6	16	7–8	6–9	18p

Teacher's editions, word cards, workbooks and wall pictures are also available.

Covers   Durable linson, attractively printed in full colour.

Printing   Excellent; clear type graded 24pt. to 12pt. Eye-catching page layout.

Illustrations   Brightly coloured and in a beautiful style.

Vocabulary   Controlled; twenty new words introduced in Book 1; thirty new words in Book 2. The vocabulary of the Platform Readers uses that of the basic books with the addition of a few 'clue' words introduced with illustrations at the beginning of each book. Sentences are restricted to one line in Books 1 to 3 and are kept structurally simple in Books 4 and 5. Word lists and word-building lists are provided at the end of each book.

Appraisal   This is an exceptionally attractive reading scheme which although designed for infants, has a high enough interest appeal for use with children up to nine
years of age who are late in learning to read. Stories in the early books are about
children and their pets, at home and at play. Book 4 contains mostly animal stories
and Book 5, which is particularly useful, draws upon a much wider context for its
original and amusing stories. There are useful word-building and phonic exercises
incorporated in the text of the first four readers.
The Platform Readers are delightful. The imaginative stories and enchanting illustrations will catch the attention of the most depressed reader. Such titles as
'Little Red Wing' and 'The Car Race' have proved amongst the most useful supplementary books for very poor young readers and retain their popularity over the
years.

THE GRIFFIN PIRATE STORIES and THE DRAGON PIRATE STORIES

Sheila K. McCullagh, MA   (E. J. Arnold)

BOYS AND GIRLS	pp.	RA	IA	Price
Book 1: The Three Pirates	16	5—6	7—12	18p
Book 2: The Blue Pirate Sails				23p
Book 3: Roderick the Red	48	5½—6½		23p
Book 4: Gregory the Green	32			
Book 5: The Storm	32	6—7		
Book 6: The Three Pirates Meet				
Book 7: The Griffin	32	6½—7½		
Book 8: On the Island				
Book 9: The Mirror, the Candle and the Flute	32	7—8		
Book 10: The Fight with the Black Pirates	48			
Book 11: The Island of the Mer-People	32	7½—8½		
Book 12: Acrooacree	48			
Workbook for Stories 1 & 2	32	5—6		19p
Workbook for Stories 3 & 4		5½—6½		
Workbook for Stories 5 & 6		6—7		
Workbook for Stories 7 & 8		6½—7½		
Workbook for Stories 9 & 10		7—8		
Workbook for Stories 11 & 12		7½—8½		
Dragon Pirate Stories				
A series (five titles)	36—48	6—7	7—12	23p—38p
B series (five titles)	48—52	6½—7½		
C series (five titles)	48—52	7—8		
D series (five titles)	64—68	7½—8½		

Covers   Readers: Gaily printed, coloured linson with stitched backs. Workbooks:
printed coloured paper.

Printing   Excellent; very clear type graded 18pt. to 12pt. Pages arranged in very
small units of text interspersed with relevant illustrations

Illustrations Readers: frequent, high quality, coloured and monochrome sketches reproduced in finely worked litho, which are outstanding both artistically and in their appeal to pupils' interest. The pirates have the genial ferocity of a comic opera.
Workbooks: frequent black and white sketches which are sometimes indistinct.

Vocabulary Controlled and graded, but rather heavily loaded in the early books.

Appraisal Because of its attractive production and its unusual and interesting subject matter (three comic pirates in search of buried treasure on the mysterious island of Acrooacree), this scheme is valuable with younger backward readers who reject the more domestic stories found in most infant readers. The workbooks provide adequate follow-up activities, games and some phonic training. Supplementary material is provided by the Dragon Books which include some more stories of the pirates and also introduce other themes in similar settings. The basic, slightly mystical atmosphere remains the same and may become boring to some children if they are required to read through the whole programme without a change.

THE GINGER BOOKS K. C. Briand (Ward, Lock)

BOYS AND GIRLS	pp.	RA	IA	Price
Introducing Ginger	14	5—6	7—10	
Book 1: Ginger Finds the Magic Ring	24			
Book 2: Ginger and the Pirates	28	5½—6½	7—10	75p the set
Book 3: Ginger at the Seaside	28			
Book 4: Ginger and the Indians	24	6—7	7—10	
Book 5: Ginger with the Mounties	32	6½—7½	7—10	
Book 6: Ginger Helps the Circus	32			
Puzzle Book 1	12	5½—6½	7—10	8p
Puzzle Book 2	12	6—7	7—10	8p

Covers Printed, coloured linson; stitched backs.

Printing Excellent. 24pt. sans-serif type. Clear page layout with each sentence printed as a separate unit.

Illustrations Cheerful cartoons printed in black and two colours. Ginger emerges as an attractive urchin.

Vocabulary Carefully controlled. Twenty five words in the Introductory Book; twenty-nine words in Book 1; similar rate of introduction in each book up to thirty-two new words in Book 6. Word lists are provided at the back of each book. Very simple sentence structure.

Appraisal Children who do not start to read until they are over seven years of age need different material from that provided in most infant reading schemes. Their interests are wider and their tastes more sophisticated. The 'Ginger Books' are a good attempt at providing for such children. They are interesting, colourful and amusing. By the subtle introduction of an acceptable amount of magic (but not imsy-whimsy fairy stuff), the author has linked the child's immediate environment with a variety of stimulating experiences including a visit to the Canadian Mounties, and a trip to a desert island by aeroplane.

The non-expendable Puzzle Books provide various activities to test word recognition and comprehension but are too slight and not sufficiently parallelled in difficulty to the readers to make them entirely successful. This is an unusual series of books that is of utmost value to teachers of seven-to-ten-year-olds whose classes include small groups of non-readers needing special treatment and materials.

MIKE AND MANDY READERS   M. Durward   (Nelson)

BOYS AND GIRLS	pp.	RA	IA	Price
Books 1—4	32	5—6	7—12	18p
Books 5—8		6—7		
Books 9—12		7—8		

Covers   Printed, coloured linson.

Printing   Excellent. Type graded 14pt. to 12pt for main text with exercises in slightly smaller type. Attractive page layout with the exercise pages particularly well designed.

Illustrations   Spirited pictures in a vivid, unusual style, printed in monochrome with colour accents. A half-page plate on every page of text; small line drawings on exercise pages.

Vocabulary   Controlled; thirty nine words introduced in Book 1; forty-six new words in Book 2. Simple direct sentences. Word lists and word building lists at the back of each book.

Appraisal   This delightful series of readers is intended for the child starting to read at seven years or more. The central characters, Mike and Mandy, emerge as real personalities and their adventures are fun as well as being well within the realms of possibility. The author exploits the everyday experiences of most children—home, school, stations, circuses and aerodromes—to produce stories that are stimulating and yet employ simple vocabulary which is immediately useful in other reading spheres. In the early books, the vocabulary load is a little heavy for the rather small amount of reading matter and a few more pages in each book without introducing more new words or a series of supplementary readers would be an advantage.

Titles include
Book 1: Mike and Mandy Go to School
Book 3: The Monkeys Get Out
Book 8: The Secret of Green Dragon.

START AFRESH READERS   C. F. Butcher   (Hulton Educational Press)

BOYS AND GIRLS	pp.	RA	IA	Price
Book 1: Tom, Dick and June	32	5½—6½	7—10	22p
Book 2: Tom, Dick and June at Play		6—7		
Book 3: Tom, Dick and June at Home		6—7		
Book 4: Tim, the Big, Black Dog		6½—7½		
Book 5: The Truck Race				
Book 6: Adventure by the Canal		7—8		

Covers   Very brightly coloured, printed and illustrated linson.

Printing   Good; clear 14pt. serif type carefully arranged in small reading units. Blocks of colour are used to delineate sections of the stories and the comprehension exercises are boxed to separate them from the text.

Illustrations   Rather scratchy, but pleasant drawings in two-colour litho. Two or three on every page interspersed amongst the text.

Vocabulary   Severely controlled and restricted. After a rather heavy load of 85 words in 32 pages in Book 1, the grading is very slight, with an average of 60 new words being introduced in each book.

Appraisal   Making a new start in reading is a stressful situation for the child who has failed to keep up with his peers in the infants' school. It is essential that the books provided for such youngsters are acceptable in appearance, subject matter and method of approach and in accordance with the maturing social and emotional status of their intended readers. These books fulfil amost all of these conditions and have the added advantage of being so carefully graded that even the slowest learner has a chance of assimilating the vocabulary and enjoying a modicum of success.
Starting in a domestic atmosphere, the stories gradually expand in both complexity and background. The final book is a simple but exciting adventure story. Some comprehension exercises are provided, but the series would be improved by the inclusion of either more and varied exercises on extra pages within the books or by inexpensive expendable workbooks.

WIDE RANGE READERS   F. J. Schonell, P. Flowerdew and A. Elliott-Cannon   (Oliver and Boyd)

BOYS AND GIRLS
Two parallel series (Green and Blue) each consisting of six readers and Quiz Books, graded as follows:

	pp.	RA	IA	Price
Book 1	144	7–8	7–10	33p
Quiz Book 1	28			13p
Book 2	144	7½–8½		33p
Quiz Book 2	28			13p
Book 3	144	8–9		33p
Quiz Book 3	28			13p
Book 4	160	8½–9½	8–12	35p
Quiz Book 4	28			13p
Book 5	192	9–10	9–14	38p
Quiz Book 5				18p
Book 6	208	9½–10½		38p
Quiz Book 6				18p

Quiz Books with answers are available, at 18p & 20p each

Interest Readers

Book 1	120	7–8	7–10	33p
Book 2	120	8–9		33p
Book 3	136	9–10	8–14	38p
Book 4	138	10–11		43p

Covers   Readers and Interest Books: Illustrated, cloth covered boards. Quiz books: linen-faced paper.

Printing   Excellent; type easy to read and graded 14pt to 10pt. Eye-catching page layout, particularly in the Interest Books.

Illustrations   Black, white and colour in the readers; black and white sketches in the Quiz Books and extremely beautiful full colour in the Interest Books.

Vocabulary   Restricted and carefully graded with plenty of purposeful repetition, very ingeniously introduced. Sentences graded in length and difficulty of structure.

Appraisal   Planned as a follow-on to the 'Happy Venture' series, these books can be used with many different ages and with children who are making normal progress or who are falling behind in reading. The first three readers contain mostly stories, but in the later books factual material is introduced. The new Interest Books offer a similar variety of articles and stories but are rather more sophisticated and modern in approach. The standard of writing is uniformly high, the books having definite literary merit in spite of the restrictions imposed upon the authors by grading of vocabulary and structure. The new Quiz Books provide useful comprehension exercises but are a trifle monotonous in their limited choice of activities.

Supplementary Reading Material for Younger Children

Young children need extensive practice in reading short, simple books on a variety of subjects if they are to gain the necessary experience with words, phrases and grammatical constructions to enable them to develop into fluent, competent readers. Most of the books in this section have been written with the needs of children making normal progress in view, but they have been selected because they appeal to a wide age range and their subject matter, format and general appearance make them particularly suitable for use with pupils who are slower to learn than most and who need extra encouragement to try their limited skills.

DOCTOR FOBBINS READERS   A. C. & E. M. Smith   (Macmillan)

BOYS AND GIRLS	pp.	RA	IA	Price
Book 1	10	5—6	7—12	10p each
Books 2—4	16	6—7		70p per set
Books 5—7	16	6½—7½		

Covers   Coloured card.

Printing   Good; type graded 24pt. to 14pt.

Illustrations   Very funny line drawings

Vocabulary   Severely restricted and graded.

Appraisal   It is difficult to be original and genuinely humorous with a severely restricted vocabulary, but, in this instance, the authors have succeeded in producing a series which is completely different, amusing and quite delightful. The adventures of that robust personality, Dr. Fobbin, and the inhabitants of an unidentified and most peculiar forest should whet the appetite of the most reluctant readers. Too slight for a complete reading scheme, these books make excellent supplementary material.

READING WITH RHYTHM   J. Taylor & T. Ingelby   (Longmans)

BOYS AND GIRLS	pp.	RA	IA	Price
Set 1: four booklets	16	5½—6½	6—9	45p per set
Set 2: four booklets		6—7		
Set 3: four booklets		6—7		
Set 4: three booklets	24	6½—7½		
Set 5: three booklets		6½—7½		
Complete set of eighteen booklets				

Covers   Stiff, coloured paper with taped backs.

Printing   Excellent; 18pt. sans-serif type with text arranged in a few short lines under the illustration on each page.

Illustrations   Bold, imaginative pictures, reproduced in full colour, which expand and help the understanding of the limited reading.

Vocabulary   Restricted; makes use of the folksong device of the recurring rhythmic refrain to help consolidate vocabulary and assist reading fluency.

Appraisal   Every class library in the lower primary school needs plenty of material like these bright little books to provide practice and pleasure for those who are having difficulty in learning to read with ease.

BEGINNING TO READ BOOKS   Various authors   (Ernest Benn)

BOYS AND GIRLS	pp.	RA	IA	Price
Thirty two titles	32	6—8	6—10	40p & 45p

Some titles available in ITA and paperback (15p)

Covers   Linen-faced, paper-covered boards with highly coloured dust jackets.

Printing   Excellent. Clear 18pt. type.

Illustrations   Each book is carefully and lavishly illustrated in an individual style. There is a half-page block on every page and the pictures are beautifully reproduced in full-colour litho.

Vocabulary   Severely restricted. The vocabulary load varies from approximately 144 different words in the easiest books to about 370 different words in the hardest ones.

Appraisal   Although designed primarily for young children making normal school progress, because of their freshness, both in subject matter and format, these books will appeal to most youngsters in the primary grades. The characters are varied and all the stories are lively and full of surprising action.

Titles include:
The Boy Who Could Not Say His Name
Grandpa's Balloon   Gordon's Go-Kart   Rainbow Pavement

THE DOLPHIN BOOKS   Ed. B. Taylor   (University of London Press)

BOYS AND GIRLS	pp.	RA	IA	Price
A Grade: twelve titles	16	6–7	6–10	10p
B Grade: twelve titles	32	7–8	7–10	15p
C Grade: twelve titles	32	7½–8½	7–10	15p
D Grade: twelve titles	48	8–9	8–12	20p
E Grade: six titles	64	8½–9½	8–12	23p
F Grade: six titles	78	9–10	8–14	25p
G Grade: six titles	96	9–10	8–14	28p
H Grade: six titles	112	10–11	8–14	30p

Covers   Stiff printed paper or linson with attractive illustrations in natural colours.

Printing   Excellent; 18 pt type in A Grade series; 12 pt. in others. Attractive page layout.

Illustrations   Eye-catching, excellently reproduced water-colours in bright tints. The work of a talented team of versatile artists.

Vocabulary   Restricted and graded. Sentence structure and paragraph length are also carefully graded in difficulty. Lively appealing styles of writing.

Appraisal   This outstanding graded series is almost a school library in itself, so varied is its coverage and interest. Designed for children making normal progress, it will have wide use with retarded readers, being colourful and attractive and having a variety of interesting and amusing stories. These cover such subjects as trains, animals, vintage cars, country life and science fiction. They are written by such well-known authors of childrens' books as Freda Collins and Andre Ducker and are of uniformly high literary standard.

Titles include:

A Grade	B Grade
Three White Mice	The Mystery Garden
The Dancing Van	Wings for Pinky
C Grade	D Grade
Rescue in the Snow	Muddy the Football
The Pebble Nest	Jenny From Ireland

E Grade	F Grade
Martin's Holiday	A Dog for Richard
The Magic Journey	Anny
G Grade	H Grade
Moon Venturer	Singapore Story
The Gay Dolphin	Silvertip

THE WILD WEST READERS   C. C. Prothero   (Wheaton)

BOYS	pp.	RA	IA	Price
Books 1, 2, 5, 6	16	6½–7½	7–10	8p
Books 7–8	24	7–8	7–10	10p
Books 9–12	32	7–8	7–10	15p

Covers   Coloured linson printed with cowboy symbols.

Printing   Fair. 18pt. type. Pages have a slightly crowded appearance.

Illustrations   Black and white sketches of little artistic merit.

Vocabulary   Restricted; elementary sentence structure.

Appraisal   These simple books have proved to be popular supplementary material for very retarded readers who will not accept the more conventional types of reading material. They use the standard situations of a western film at a very simple level, the stories being naive to adults but apparently immensely enjoyable to younger readers. Activities and simple exercises are included to help teach the vocabulary used in the stories and to check comprehension.

Titles include:

The Store in Town	The Robber of Red Valley
Pete the Outlaw	The Rodeo

BEGINNER BOOKS   Various authors   (Collins)

BOYS AND GIRLS	pp.	RA	IA	Price
Thirty-six titles	64	6–8	5–12	50p

Covers   Illustrated, paper-covered boards

Printing   Excellent. 24pt. type; unconventional page layout with striking patterns made from the arrangements of blocks of text and illustrations.

Illustrations   These are picture stories and the illustrations by an outstanding team of artists are largely responsible for the astonishing attraction of the books.

Vocabulary   Severely restricted; ranging from fifty new words per book to approximately three hundred.

Appraisal   This series includes several books by Dr. Seuss who might be described as the genius of the controlled vocabulary. He takes faithful old teaching words like 'hat' and 'cat' and weaves them into the incredible adventures of the 'Cat in the Hat' and other unlikely creatures. Until you have read them, you cannot believe how funny they are! Other books in the series are good, even if not up to this unusual standard, and all will give pleasure to those lucky enough to have them in their class libraries.

Titles include:

The Diggingest Dog	Green Eggs and Ham
Chitty Chitty Bang Bang	A Fly Went By

READ BY READING   J. Taylor and T. Ingelby   (Longmans)

BOYS AND GIRLS	pp.	RA	IA	Price
Set 1: Orange Books—four				
titles	16	6½–7½	7–10	60p per set
Set 2: Green Books—four				
titles	24	7–8		£1.65 per
Set 3: Blue Books—four				complete set
titles	24	7½–8½		of 12

Covers   Stiff, coloured card with taped backs.

Printing   Excellent. 18pt. type with sentences arranged in small units around well-placed illustrations.

Illustrations   Frequent half and full-page plates in a bold, slightly grotesque style with considerable eye appeal. Well reproduced in full colour.

Vocabulary   Restricted, with plenty of rhythmic repetition to aid reading fluency. Some of the proper names and the odd difficult word may provide stumbling blocks for slower readers.

Appraisal   These books are well devised, attractive and hard-wearing, but, alas, no longer as inexpensive as when first published. They are short enough to be read in one sitting by even the most discouraged reader and make first class supplementary readers for younger children.

Titles include:

Set 1: Three Wicked Goats	The Hero
Set 2: Granny's Three Black Cats	
Set 3: Simon's Zoo	Zarifa, the Camel

THE SIGNAL BOOKS   C. Niven   (Methuen Educational)

BOYS AND GIRLS	pp.	RA	IA	Price
The Helicopter Dog	16	7–8	7–10	17p
Lost at Sea				
Donkey Goes for a Swim				
The Runaway Lion	16	7½–8½	7–10	17p
The Vanishing Children				
Danger at the Zoo				

Covers   Illustrated, linen-faced card; stapled backs.

Printing   Excellent; clear 18pt. serif type, carefully arranged in short units.

Illustrations   Bold, brightly coloured pictures, well reproduced in three-colour litho. Half-page plate on every page.

Vocabulary   Restricted and slightly graded, but rather heavily loaded with word classes for such short books (only 12 pages of story per book). Word and Phrase picture dictionaries are included on the last four pages of each book.

Appraisal   These simple, unsophisticated stories will be appreciated by children in primary school who are just beginning to read for pleasure, and by some older children in ESN classes. Being attractive to look at, very short and with uncomplicated plots, they can be coped with by many children without the concentration or perseverence to read anything more complex.

FLAMINGO BOOKS   Various authors   (Oliver & Boyd)

BOYS AND GIRLS	pp.	RA	IA	Price
First Year Pink	16	7–8	6–10	10p
First Year Red	16	7½–8½	6–10	10p
Second Year Pink	32	7½–8½	7–12	15p
Second Year Red	32	8–9	7–12	15p
Third Year Pink	32	8–9	7–12	15p
Third Year Red	40–48	8½–9½	8–12	20p
Fourth Year Pink	40–48	9–10	8–12	20p
Fourth Year Red	48	9–10	8–12	20p

Four titles in each section

Covers   Brightly coloured, illustrated card.

Printing   Excellent; type graded 18pt. to 12pt.

Vocabulary   Restricted and graded.

Appraisal   This pleasant series has recently been doubled in size. It is designed for youngsters making normal progress and provides a charming selection of original stories by a team of well-known authors. The scope is so wide and the subject matter so varied that the books make excellent supplementary readers for classes with a wide distribution of reading ability.

Titles include:

Matilda	The Fish and Chips Van	Wolf Baby
The Fisher Boy	Jonathan	The Antonios Alone

JUNIOR READING SERIES   Various authors   (Frederick Muller)

BOYS AND GIRLS	pp.	RA	IA	Price
Eight titles	32	7½–8½	7–10	50p

Cover   Fully illustrated, paper-covered boards.

Printing   Excellent; a variety of type faces and sizes are used, but in most cases the text is subsidiary to the illustrations.

Illustrations   At least one large picture on every page, in a variety of styles and techniques. All are of high artistic standard and beautifully reproduced in rich colours.

Vocabulary   Unrestricted and at times the very slight amount of reading is heavily loaded with unusual words.

Appraisal   These books are not included so much because they are easy to read but because they are ideal for being read to small groups of slow-learning children and for encouraging that 'looking at books' which is an essential preliminary to wanting to learn to read. The stories are unusual, simple in concept yet written in rich language and the illustrations are delightful. The books are a natural invitation to any young child to hurry up and learn to read for himself.

Titles include:

Johnny and the Monarch
The Man Who Walked Round the World

Next Door to Laura Linda
Will You Carry Me?

School Library Books:
Adventure and Other Stories

School libraries tend to cater mainly for the brighter child and for the better reader. They frequently neglect to provide suitable books for those pupils who are reluctant to make profitable use of library periods because their limited skills make reading hard work instead of a relaxation. The series included in this section have been chosen especially to encourage such children, particularly those in the upper classes of primary schools and in the slower streams of secondary schools. The criteria for choice have been a wide range of interest level, including, where possible, subjects of particular interest to children with non-academic outlooks, combined with a simplicity of language and of syntax.

BANDIT BOOKS   Various authors   (Ernest Benn Ltd.)

BOYS	pp.	RA	IA	Price
One Star Books: two titles	120	7—8	9—16	45p
Regular Books: three titles	120	8—9	9—16	45p

Covers   Linen-faced, paper-covered boards.

Printing   Good; 12pt. type; conventional novel-like layout.

Illustrations   Occasional black and white sketches.

Vocabulary   Severely restricted to five hundred specially chosen words in One Star Books; restricted in others.

Appraisal   These stories will go some way to filling the need for school library books within the capacity of slower readers. They will appeal to many boys, being exciting, imaginative and well written. At the same time, the vocabulary and sentence structure are such that any child with a reading age of approximately eight years can read and enjoy them.

Titles include:

One Star Books:	Killer Road	Art and the Sounders
Regular Books:	Sandy Smith	Tony and the Secret Money
		The Camp in the Hills

THE WINDRUSH BOOKS   Various authors   (Oxford University Press)

BOYS AND GIRLS	pp.	RA	IA	Price
Books 1—6	64	8—9	10—16	30p
Books 7—8	72			35p

Covers   Coloured, linen-faced, paper-covered boards.

Printing   Excellent. Very clear 14pt. type with a well-planned page layout which avoids any suggestion of an infant reader.

Illustrations   Frequent black and white sketches.

Vocabulary   Restricted.

Appraisal   Using a severely limited vocabulary and a very simple presentation, the authors of these original stories have made an outstanding contribution to the material available to older children with limited reading ability. The development of character within the uncomplicated but unusual plots is exceptionally good. The young people in these stories breathe the same air as their readers and grow convincingly in spite of the literary restrictions placed upon the authors. The choice of background is often unfamiliar—for instance, that of 'Bill Thompson's Pigeon' depicts life in the industrial north of England during the depression of the 1930s—and they are vividly presented so as to add much to the value of the tales. It is rare to find such good writing in material prepared especially for poor readers. This series is a 'must' for school libraries.

Titles include:

The Rescue and the Poisoned Dog   Gypsy Hill Joe
The Lifeboat Haul and Elizabeth Woodcock

JETS　　Various authors　　(Jonathan Cape)

BOYS AND GIRLS	pp.	RA	IA	Price
Twelve titles	112–128	8–9	12–18	50p library
				25–30p p/back

Covers　Illustrated and brightly coloured card; rather insecure binding which will not stand up to rough handling.

Printing　Good; clear 12pt. type; some pages rather over-crowded.

Vocabulary　Restricted; very simple sentence structure and uncomplicated style.

Appraisal　This is a series of gay, easy stories intended as leisure reading for teenagers. It should be good bait to attract those pupils in their last years at school who still regard reading as an arduous duty rather than a relaxation. These stories are lively and up-to-date; the characters are mainly young people just starting to learn their first jobs; the plots are concerned with the problems they have to face. Mixed up with the story-telling is a surprising amount of palatably presented common-sense! All-in-all, the mixture is ideal and cannot help but be popular with most youngsters without academic leanings.

Titles include:
Sally of St. Patrick's	Skid Pan
Half-Day Thursday	The Four Aces

ENGLISH PICTURE CLASSICS　　Various editors　　(Oxford University Press)

BOYS AND GIRLS	pp.	RA	IA	Price
Eleven titles	128	9–10	12–16	18p–25p

Covers　Stiff linson, printed with coloured illustrations.

Printing　Good; clear 10pt. type; excellent page layout.

Illustrations　Black and white sketches by a team of versatile artists with distinctive styles. Eight full-page plates and smaller illustrations on nearly every page. Attractive end-plates introduce the characters in the stories.

Vocabulary　Slightly restricted; glossaries of difficult words at the end of each book. Simplified sentence structure.

Appraisal　These abridged versions of well-known novels are excellent of their type and are popular with older backward readers. The abridging has been skilfully done; the books read as fast-moving tales with much direct speech. They unfold as a coherent whole, although inevitably there has been loss in characterization and background detail. These books will introduce many children to good stories which they would be incapable of appreciating in their original form.

Titles include:
Treasure Island	Lorna Doone
Robinson Crusoe	Jane Eyre

STREAMLINE BOOKS　　Various authors　　(Nelson)

BOYS AND GIRLS	pp.	RA	IA	Price
Seventeen titles	88–114	9–10	10–adult	23p–25p

Covers   Stiff, coloured card.

Printing   Good; clear 12 pt. type; conventional layout.

Illustrations   Occasional black and white sketches interspersed amongst the text.

Vocabulary   Carefully restricted to approximately 2000 different words per volume.

Appraisal   It is pleasant to find a series of paper-backs designed exclusively for the older but poorer reader. This is an especially good collection of simplified versions of well-known books. The editor has been unconventional in his choice, avoiding the more usual classical material and using instead exciting, modern books such as first-rate detective stories. These books, however, are not simply condensed and emasculated versions of the originals. Instead, they have been carefully re-written with simplified language and sentence structure yet preserving the continuity of the originals and as much as possible of their atmosphere and style.

Titles include:
Five Red Herrings (based on the novel by Dorothy M. Sayers)
Trent's Last Case (based on the novel by E. C. Bentley)

THE JOAN TATE BOOKS   J. Tate   (Heinemann)

GIRLS	**pp.**	**RA**	**IA**	**Price**
Eighteen titles	60	9—10	10—18	18p

Covers   Printed, illustrated paper.

Printing   Good; clear 10pt. type; typical paper-back format and layout.

Illustrations   Several black and white sketches in each book.

Vocabulary   Slightly restricted.

Appraisal   The author of these out-of-the-ordinary stories, in endeavouring to provide acceptable reading for older girls with few academic interests, has got right away from the conventional middle-class atmosphere of many girls' books. She has written simple stories about the type of child who is likely to be reading books at this level, has set them firmly in an urban working-class environment and has made the main characters girls either just about to leave school or working in their first jobs. All the various colours and races that are found in such places are included. Their problems are worked out against a background of secondary modern schools, milk bars and the greyness of industrial England. This series is a good addition to the school library.

Titles include: Picture Charlie   Lucy   Coal Happy

SHORTER CLASSICS   Ed. M. W. & G. Thomas   (Ginn)

BOYS AND GIRLS	**pp.**	**RA**	**IA**	**Price**
Twenty-five titles	160—192	9—11	10—adult	43p

Covers   Printed, cloth-covered boards.

Printing   Excellent; 10pt. type. Very carefully arranged page layout which is particularly easy to read.

Illustrations   Black and white; many full-page plates in each book.

Vocabulary Much simplified compared with the originals but still difficult for genuinely retarded readers.

Appraisal A series of carefully arranged and edited classics, these books are ideal class material for slower learners in secondary schools. They preserve much of the feeling of the original books, but at the same time reduce complications of plot and stylistic difficulties, so that they become understandable to those who could not cope with the originals.

Titles include:

For the Term of his Natural Life	Barnaby Rudge
Moby Dick	The Talisman

ACTIVE READERS   Various authors   (Ginn)

BOYS AND GIRLS	pp.	RA	IA	Price
First series: sixteen titles	160–176	9–11	8–16	40p
Second Series: four titles	168–192	10–12	8–16	40p

Covers Cloth covered hardboards.

Printing Good; clear attractive page layout.

Illustrations Striking black and white drawings, including some full page plates.

Vocabulary Some restriction, but there is a considerable difference in difficulty among the books. Effectiveness of style also varies, but in most volumes it is direct and vigorous with considerable literary merit.

Appraisal Older backward readers who have obtained some proficiency in the mechanics of reading will like these action-packed yarns, well illustrated and, generally speaking, well written in simple prose. Many of the stories could well be linked with social studies. 'Young Mounties', for instance gives an excellent picture of life among the Eskimos of Northern Canada, whilst 'X-bar-Y Ranch' is a story of early nineteenth-century pioneers in Western America. A recent addition has as its theme the transportation of convicts to Australia.
Each book contains practical exercises based on the text. These exercises require the minimum of writing but challenge the pupils' ingenuity and powers of observation.
Although these books have been available for a considerable time, they are still valuable additions to the school library, being suitable for almost all children in the upper primary school as well as being appreciated by the slower readers.

Titles include:

First Series:	*Second Series:*
Goodbye to the Bush	Friends Divided

THE KENNETT LIBRARY   Ed. J. Kennett   (Blackie)

BOYS AND GIRLS	pp.	RA	IA	Price
Short Series: nineteen titles	100	9–11	10–16	38p
Long Series: fifteen titles	170	10–12	10–16	45p
Modern Series: two titles				47p

Covers Coloured, glossy paper-covered boards, illustrated on the front cover.

Printing Good; 10pt. type; clear page layout.

Illustrations Sketches in black, white and red; Four full page plates in each book.

Vocabulary   Simplified sentence structure and clear straightforward style with reduced vocabulary. The books are slightly graded in difficulty.

Appraisal   At the present time, there are several series of restricted versions of famous novels available. Some are better than others but all serve the purpose of introducing to reluctant readers the great books which are the heritage of the English-speaking world. The editor of the 'Kennett Library' has done an honest job. He has cut relentlessly, shearing the books of most description and extraneous detail, yet leaving bright, intelligible narrative which retains some of the atmosphere of the originals. The books deserve a place in any school library, as they will be read and enjoyed by many who would turn away from the originals.

Titles include:

Short Series:	Long Series:
Westward Ho!	Dr. Jekyll and Mr. Hyde
Ben Hur	Adventures of Tom Sawyer

SIMPLIFIED ENGLISH SERIES   Ed. C. K. Williams   (Longmans)

BOYS AND GIRLS	**pp.**	**RA**	**IA**	**Price**
Sixty-one titles	96—122	10—12	14—adult	19p

Covers   Coloured paper.

Printing   Good; clear 10pt. type. Occasionally pages are a little crowded in appearance.

Illustrations   Three or four full-page plates in black and white in each book.

Vocabulary   Severely restricted to the level of the two thousand root words of 'A General Service List of English Words'[1]. A few colourful words outside this range have been retained to preserve the flavour of the original text, but are explained by footnotes when necessary.

Appraisal   With more and more pupils staying at school after fifteen years, the demand for simple material with an adult appeal increases. This series, of which the primary intention was to provide extra reading experience for young foreign students, is almost a 'must' for any comprehensive school library. The books, which cover a wide variety of subjects and styles, have been carefully edited so that the restriction of language does not make them too stilted and some of the attraction of the original work remains.

Titles include:

The Wooden Horse	The Kraken Wakes
Campbell's Kingdom	The Thirty-Nine Steps
The Moonstone	The Invisible Man

SIMPLIFIED EDITIONS OF CHILDRENS NOVELS   F. Knight
(Macmillans)

BOYS	**pp.**	**RA**	**IA**	**Price**
Bluenose Pirate	129	9—10	9—16	40p
The Golden Monkey	144			45p
Voyage to Bengal	160			35p
Clipper to China	144			35p

[1] West. M. *A General Service List of English Words.* London: Longmans, 1962.

Covers   Mantex boards, not very hard-wearing.

Printing   Good; clear 12pt. type; paragraphs well spaced out.

Illustrations   Occasional lively black and white sketches and some full-page plates and diagrams.

Vocabulary   Some restriction; many of the technical and nautical terms are far more difficult than the overall difficulty level of the whole book implies.

Appraisal   Frank Knight writes first class sea stories and, as he has done his own abridgement of these four books, they retain much of their original spirit. The books are deservedly popular with older boys. Other titles are also available.

TOPLINERS   Various authors   (Pan/Macmillan)

BOYS AND GIRLS	**pp.**	**RA**	**IA**	**Price**
Nineteen titles	112—160	10—12	14—adult	18p—20p

Covers   Printed and illustrated paper, in the rather garish tradition of the cheaper paper-back, and with its typical size, format and binding.

Printing   Fair; 12 or 10 pt. serif type; conventional page layout.

Illustrations   Most titles are unillustrated but the books by E. Hildick have cartoon-like black and white drawings occasionally.

Vocabulary   Slightly restricted, with simple sentence construction and uncomplicated paragraph structure. The styles vary from the frankly 'pop' style to the faintly mystical with a wide range of variations in between.

Appraisal   In an attempt to provide stimulating books at a competitive price for the 'reluctant reader' with slightly below average reading skills, and little interest in the books more usually found in school libraries, the publishers of this series have brought together an interesting and exciting collection of books. There is no main theme for the series and subjects vary from ghost stories, through science fiction and detective stories to tales that deal with the social problems of young people in a frank and broad-minded fashion. The quality of the stories varies, as would be expected in so large a series, but on the whole, the books are well written, with original plots, well developed characterization and contempory but reasonably acceptable literary usage.
These books present an acceptable alternative to comics and pulp magazines, and would be valuable additions to the libraries in secondary modern and comprehensive schools. They would also be useful in classes for slow-learning and educationally retarded adults.

Titles include:

Scare Power	Sam and I
The Golden Orphans	The Contender

School Library Books:
Interests and Activities

The books listed in this section are of two types. There are some which have been simply written for backward readers, dealing with the normal, practical and non-fiction interests of boys and girls between the ages of seven and sixteen years. Others are not primarily intended for backward children but have been found to be useful as sources of information which can be referred to by the better readers in the special class and can also be easily adapted by the teacher for those who are not so far advanced.

ADVENTURES IN LIFE   Jones and Saltiel   (Wheaton)

BOYS AND GIRLS	pp.	RA	IA	Price
Girls' Series Eight titles	16	7–8	8–14	10p
Boys' Series Eight titles	16	7–8	8–14	10p
Workbooks				4p

Covers   Coloured and printed linen-faced card.

Printing   Fair; 18pt. sans-serif type.

Illustrations   Half-page plates on every page, printed in two-colours.

Vocabulary   Restricted with a strong phonic bias. Phonic lists are given in each section and special interest words which may cause difficulty are listed at the end of each book.

Appraisal   Although to the adult eye these little books are not very attractive, most young people seem to enjoy reading them. They deal with the glamour professions in an idealized and superficial manner and it is perhaps unreality, bringing the seemingly impossible within the realms of possibility, that makes the books so popular, particularly with duller children.

Titles include:
Girls' Series: Ballet Dancer	Air Hostess	Show Jumper
Boys' Series: Channel Swimmer	Racing Driver	Big Game Hunter

THEY WERE FIRST   Brookfield, Newton & Smith   (Oliver & Boyd)

BOYS	pp.	RA	IA	Price
Books 1–8	16	7–8	8–14	13p

Covers   Illustrated printed linson with stapled backs.

Printing   Excellent. 24pt. sans-serif type printed rather closely but carefully arranged in short lines.

Illustrations   Dynamic pictures which emphasize the strength and courage of the people they depict and give vivid impressions of the conditions encountered in their endeavours. Several page plates in full colour and smaller plates in colour and in monochrome.

Vocabulary   Restricted. A rather heavy load of geographical terms and place names for the limited amount of reading.

Appraisal   Men who have made important contributions to our knowledge of the physical world have been chosen as the subjects of these short books. Tribute is paid to their individual initiative and heroism against a background of facts and ideas for further discussion and investigation. The books are very slight but will appeal to most older boys.

Titles include: Gagarin   Bleriot   Peary   Amundsen

WE DISCOVER BOOKS   R. H. C. Fice & I. M. Simkiss   (E. J. Arnold)

BOYS AND GIRLS	pp.	RA	IA	Price
Sixteen titles	24	7—8	7—10	25p—33p

Covers   Coloured, printed linson, illustrated with bold, eye-catching drawings.

Printing   Excellent; clear 14pt. type; pages laid out with alternate blocks of text and relevant diagrams and drawings.

Illustrations   Some photographs and many semi-diagrammatic drawings well reproduced in full-colour litho.

Vocabulary   Restricted with very simple sentence structure.

Appraisal   Designed as an introduction to general science for young children, these books explain scientific principles at a simple, practical level. They would be useful interest books for slow-learners in primary schools.

Titles include: Plants   Magnets   An Aquarium

HELP YOURSELF HANDWORK   H. E. Manistre   (Cassell)

BOYS AND GIRLS	pp.	RA	IA	Price
Books 1—12	16	8—9	10—16	30p
(Books 3, 7 o/p)				

Covers   Coloured linson.

Printing   Good; 10pt. type; very clear layout which makes it easy to follow the method of making the models.

Illustrations   Numerous diagrams in two-colour litho.

Vocabulary   Restricted. Instructions are clearly expressed and reduced to a minimum.

Appraisal   It is a good remedial technique to encourage the poor reader to exercise his skills by giving him some concrete objective. In order to make the attractive models described in these books, the pupil has to read the instructions and understand what they mean. Then he has to translate them into terms of material such as card, wood and paper. It is an approach that will appeal to many children who show little interest in ordinary books. Each book contains clearly illustrated instructions for making two models. As well as giving excellent practice in reading for instruction, the model-making involves the pupils in a great deal of practical arithmetic. These books would be a useful addition to the bookshelves of any class for slow-learners.

Titles include:
Book 1: Stage Coach   The Rocket
Book 4: Aircraft Carrier   Dredger

MEASURING AND MAKING   C. Carver and C. H. Stowasser   (Oxford University Press)

BOYS AND GIRLS	pp.	RA	IA	Price
Books 1 and 2	64	8—9	8—14	50p

Covers   Patterned paper-covered boards with spiral binding.

Printing   Excellent. 14pt. type; page layout designed to display the diagrams and instructions in a logical, easy-to-follow sequence.

Illustrations   Many diagrams which make it easy for the poor reader to follow the processes described.

Vocabulary   Restricted.

Appraisal   These books use paper-modelling to train pupils in two important learning techniques—purposeful reading for information and instruction and the relationship of practical measurement to simple geometric forms—in a manner which is likely to be palatable to those children finding education a slow and profitless business. The models suggested are ingenious, original and require little in the way of equipment and material. Yet they are simple enough to give the slowest learner a sense of accomplishment when he has succeeded in making them.

DOLPHIN SCIENCE SERIES   Various authors   (University of London Press)

BOYS AND GIRLS	pp.	RA	IA	Price
Sixteen titles	32	8—9	8—14	38p—45p

Covers   Plain, paper-covered boards with cased backs; brightly illustrated dust covers.

Printing   Good; clear 14pt. type; layout arranged with text in small units and well-spaced out.

Illustrations   Half-page plates at the top or bottom of every page in a variety of styles, some of which are very amusing; well-reproduced in full colour.

Vocabulary   Slightly restricted with lists of difficult words at the end of each book.

Appraisal   No school library is complete without plenty of simple non-fiction books to provide good general reading and material for projects and discussion groups. This series is excellent; it is simply written, provides useful and accurate information in an 'easy-to understand' form and covers a variety of subjects. Although originally intended for children making normal progress in primary schools, it would be valuable in E.S.N. classes and with all retarded readers.

Titles include: Materials   Space   Machines   Ants

FAMOUS SHIPS   Brookfield, Newton and Smith   (Oliver and Boyd)

BOYS	pp.	RA	IA	Price
Four titles	24	8—9	8—16	33p

Covers   Coloured and dramatically illustrated linson; stapled backs.

Printing   Good; 18pt. sans-serif type. The pages look over-crowded because the spacing is close for such large type.

Illustrations   Magnificent seascapes, full of action and excitement, reproduced beautifully in full-colour or monochrome litho.

Vocabulary   Slightly restricted with simple sentence structure.

Appraisal   Drawing on the heritage of British naval history, these books tell the stories of four famous ships and of the courage of the men who sailed in them. They are both inspiring and unusual additions to the school library.

Titles include: The Flying Enterprise   The Royal Charter

READ ABOUT SCIENCE   Ed. K. Gardner   (Reader's Digest, U.K.)

BOYS AND GIRLS	pp.	RA	IA	Price
Red Book and Blue Book	96	9–10	9–16	23p

Covers   Printed, illustrated, coloured linson with cased backs.

Printing   Good; clear 10pt. type; page layout similar to that used in 'Reader's Digest' magazines.

Illustrations   A variety of diagrams, sketches, maps and photographs, each high-lighting important points in the articles.

Vocabulary   Slightly restricted; important and difficult words are carefully explained in glossaries at the end of each book.

Appraisal   These science miscellanies cover a variety of topics in easily-written, rather chatty articles which are both interesting and informative, even if only at a superficial level. They make interesting reading for slower readers in secondary schools who prefer fact to fiction. Useful comprehension exercises, activities and discussion subjects are included.

SPOTLIGHT ON TROUBLE BOOKS   H. C. Gunzburg   (Methuen)

BOYS	pp.	RA	IA	Price
Eight titles	40	9–10	14–adult	13p

Covers   Printed paper; stapled backs.

Printing   10pt. type; dull and rather crowded page layout.

Illustrations   A few black and white drawings in each book.

Vocabulary   Restricted with considerable repetition.

Appraisal   The transition from the protected environment of the special school to the uninterested toughness of the outside world is a critical period for school leavers of limited intellectual ability. Realizing this, the author of these books has devised a series of situational tales intended to draw the readers' attention to some of the problems they are likely to come up against when they leave school and start work. The books are carefully and thoughtfully written, with interesting characters, realistic situations and reasonable, practical solutions to the problems.
Possibly as a result of attempts to keep down the price of books which can only have a limited market, the books are, unfortunately, drab in appearance with little about them to attract the immediate attention. Use of colour and modern layout techniques would have made them more immediately acceptable to their potential readers.

Titles include:
Trouble with the Landlady   Trouble at Work
Trouble at the Dance   Trouble with Charlie

FIFTEEN   Ed. M. Grieve   (Collins)

GIRLS		pp.	RA	IA	Price
One title		144	11–12	14–18	88p

Covers   Paper-covered boards illustrated by an attractive photograph of a fifteen-year-old girl.

Printing   Good; mainly 10pt. type with other faces and sizes used for contrast. Varied page layout with much use of eye-catching page plans and cartoon strips.

Illustrations   Plentiful black and white drawings and photographs with the emphasis always on the age group for which the book was designed.

Vocabulary   Unrestricted but simple and informal in style.

Appraisal   Designed as a simple handbook on socially acceptable behaviour for young girls about to leave school, this book combines humour, common-sense and a delicate appreciation of the needs of young people into an attractive and useful miscellany. The editor shows great understanding of the problems of growing up in a world of rapidly changing values and patterns of behaviour and offers many suggestions of ways in which ends can be achieved with the minimum of friction and upset between different age groups. Many of the articles could lead to serious class discussion.
Unfortunately the book, published originally in 1966, is already dating—the skirts are neither mini nor maxi— but it still remains a useful and interesting addition to the library. 'Sixteen', the companion volume, is similar in style and format but lays greater emphasis on the problems to be faced in adult life.

Books for Teaching Essential Reading Skills, Spelling and Basic English Usage

This section includes books designed to teach special skills such as phonic analysis and comprehension; books planned to aid general reading improvement by means of exercises and drills; and text-books designed to help children to master basic English usage. Emphasis has been placed on books suitable for use with older, slower learners which give plenty of purposeful activity both in reading and writing.

SOUND SENSE (Rev. Ed.)   A. E. Tansley, BSc., M.Ed,   (E. J. Arnold)

BOYS AND GIRLS	pp.	RA	IA	Price
Books 1 and 2	32	6—7	7—12	23p
Books 3 and 4	32	6½—7½		
Books 5 and 6	40	7—8		
Book 7	40	7½—8½		
Book 8	48	8—9		
Teacher's Booklet	24			

Covers   Brightly coloured, printed linson with a distinctive design.

Printing   Good; type graded from 14pt. sans-serif type in Book 1 to 12pt. serif type in Book 8.

Illustrations   Plentiful, well-reproduced drawings in full-colour litho.

Vocabulary   Restricted and controlled by a systematic introduction of phonic sounds in a logical sequence.

Appraisal   This set of books provides a thorough training in the recognition and use of commonly used phonic sounds in standard English. It is carefully thought out, stresses the need for comprehension as well as word-recognition, and tests learning throughout by interesting exercises and stories. It makes a valuable adjunct to other remedial reading series which do not stress phonic training.

THE ENGLISH WORKBOOKS   R. Ridout   (Ginn)

BOYS AND GIRLS	pp.	RA	IA	Price
Introductory Books 1 & 2	32	6—7	6—9	10p
Books 1 and 2	48	7—8	7—9	
Books 3 and 4	48	8—9	8—10	
Books 5 and 6	48	9—10	9—12	13p
Book 7	48	10—11	10—14	
Book 8	64	10—11	10—14	15p

Covers   White paper; foolscap size; stapled backs.

Printing   Good; graded 14pt. to 12pt type; clear, spacious layout. The books are designed to be expendable and plenty of space is provided for writing answers.

Illustrations   Black and white drawings; distribution varies from numerous with some full-page plates in Book 1 to nil in Book 8.

Vocabulary   Restricted and carefully graded; dictionaries provided at the end of each book.

Appraisal   This is a comprehensive English course suitable for use with retarded readers. It aims at improving the child's ability to write clear, correct English, at understanding what is read and at extending vocabulary. Exercises are interesting and varied. The scheme is particularly valuable to the special class teacher, as it is so designed that each child can work through it at his individual pace.

FIRST STEPS IN READING FOR MEANING   G. Carr   (University of London Press)

BOYS AND GIRLS	pp.	RA	IA	Price
Books 1—4	32	6½—7½	6—9	13p

Covers   Coloured card; stitched backs.

Printing   Excellent; clear 18pt. sans-serif type; well-designed page layout.

Illustrations   Bold pictures in black, white and three other colours.

Vocabulary   Very carefully controlled and graded. The words used would be familiar to most children who have read the first two books of any infant reading scheme.

Appraisal   Training for reading for meaning should be an integral part of all reading instruction from the very beginning. Yet apart from workbooks based on specific reading schemes, there is very little material available at a simple level. This series is a good attempt to provide supplementary training in understanding ideas expressed in print, for children with very limited reading skills. Because of the severely limited vocabulary, there is very little variety in the early books, but all the questions and activities are chosen to encourage accurate reading and intelligent interpretation of text and illustrations. These books are extremely useful with poor readers who have a tendency to 'bark at print'.

ESSENTIAL READ AND SPELL   F. J. & F. E. Schonell   (Macmillan)

BOYS AND GIRLS	pp.	RA	IA	Price
Book 1	72	7—8	7—10	33p
Book 2	80	8—9	8—12	
Book 3	72	9—10	9—12	
Book 4	78	10—11	10—12	
Teacher's Book				40p

Covers   Printed linson.

Printing   Good. The text uses bold, ordinary and italic faces in both 14pt. and 12pt. type to give emphasis and variety to the layout. Pages are arranged in pairs with spelling words grouped at the top of each left-hand page with an illustrative story beneath, and the relevant exercises are attractively arranged on the right-hand page.

Illustrations   Well-reproduced pictures in two-colour litho.

Vocabulary   Carefully restricted. The spelling words are taken from the 'Essential Spelling List' (Schonell, 1951) and are carefully integrated into the text and exercises to give the pupils the maximum meaningful practice in reading and writing them.

Appraisal   Experienced teachers in classes for slow-learning children have found these books an attractive approach to the teaching of spelling, particularly when the children are also having trouble with reading. The illustrations and stories help to sustain interest and the varied exercises are such that the pupils can read them unaided and work at their own speed with the minimum of supervision. The spelling words are carefully chosen and graded, and their arrangement into phonic groups is particularly helpful.

SELF-HELP ENGLISH   R. Ridout   (Macmillan)

BOYS AND GIRLS	pp.	RA	IA	Price
Introductory Book	64	7—8	9—12	16p
Book 1	96	8—9	9—12	25p
Book 2	112	9—10	10—14	30p
Book 3	128	10—11	10—14	30p
Book 4	128	11—12	10—16	25p

Covers   Manilla printed with an attractive design; book size 8 x 6½ ins.

Printing   Good; outstanding page layout.

Illustrations   Black and white drawings introduced to make the exercises more interesting and easier to understand. Some are very amusing.

Vocabulary   Restricted and graded. Miniature dictionaries provided at each level.

Appraisal   This English course is designed especially for backward children. It aims at developing independence in the writing of English by providing in a simple, interesting fashion, all the material that the pupil needs to make grammatically acceptable responses to the various questions, activities and puzzles. The books are particularly good in helping to extend written vocabulary.

APPROACH TO NUMBER   D. H. Gale   (Hulton Educational Press)

BOYS AND GIRLS	pp.	RA	IA	Price
Number Readiness				
Books 1—4	16	7—8	6—10	19p
Workbooks 1 and 2	14			16p
Number Language				
Books 1—4	24	8—9	7—14	26p
Books 5—6	28			29p
The Teaching of Number	56			56p
(Teacher's Handbook)				

Covers   Number Readiness: printed, coloured card. Number Language: coloured linson.

Printing   Good. Number Readiness: Books 1-2, 24pt. bold type; Books 3-4, 18pt. bold type. Number Language: 14pt. bold type. Printed in two colours with interesting page layout.

Vocabulary   Restricted; limited mostly to words commonly used in primary school arithmetic.

Appraisal   These books have been included in this section as they teach the essential skill of using and understanding the vocabulary of number. They are not concerned so much with the teaching of arithmetic as with the words and concepts that must be understood if a child is to make the developmental change from the concrete experience of number to its abstract appreciation. From this point of view they make an excellent series, as they review systematically, in an interesting and easily comprehensible fashion, most of the terms a child is likely to need if he is going to tackle elementary mathematics successfully. The books not only attempt to familiarize the child with relevant vocabulary but also to illustrate clearly the concepts that are symbolized by such words. They will be particulary helpful with slow-learning children in special schools and for children who are culturally deprived.

WORD PERFECT   R. Ridout   (Ginn)

BOYS AND GIRLS	pp.	RA	IA	Price
Introductory Book	32	5—6	5—10	15p
Book 1	48	6—7	6—10	19p
Book 2	48	7—8	7—11	19p
Book 3	48	7½—8½	7—11	19p
Book 4	48	8—9	8—12	19p
Book 5	64	8½—9½	8—12	23p
Book 6	64	9—10	8—14	23p
Book 7	96	10—12	8—14	30p
Book 8: All About English Words	208	12—14	10—adult	53p
Teacher's Manual	112			43p

Covers   Coloured, printed linson.

Printing   Excellent; Introductory and Book 1: mixed 14pt. and 12pt. type; other books: mixed 12pt. and 10pt. type. Attractive, spacious page layout with exercises clearly defined.

Illustrations   Frequent, simple black and white drawings which add interest to the spelling lists.

Vocabulary   Graded, carefully chosen spelling lists, with a slight, phonic bias. Instructions for exercises are very simply phrased.

Appraisal   This is a spelling and vocabulary extension scheme based on the theory put forward by the author that 'the grouping of words according to common structural elements does facilitate their learning.' It is an active scheme demanding far more from the pupil than the mere parrot-learning of lists of words and is extremely useful in helping poor readers and spellers who are making a new start. Book 8 is a comprehensive reference book which would be useful for all secondary school pupils whatever their learning capacity.

BETTER ENGLISH   R. Ridout   (Ginn)

BOYS AND GIRLS	pp.	RA	IA	Price
Introductory Book	64	7—8	7—10	25p
Book 1	64	7½—8½	7—10	25p
Book 2	96	8—9	8—12	33p
Book 3	96	8½—9½	8—12	33p
Book 4	128	9—10	8—14	38p
Book 5	160	10—11	9—14	40p
Index to all books	16			3p

Covers   Brightly coloured, printed linson with an original alphabet motif.

Printing   Good; very clear print graded 14pt. to 12pt. Some pages, in Book 2 particularly, have a crowded appearance. Coloured backgrounds are used effectively to differentiate sections of the exercises.

Illustrations   Gaily coloured, cheerful pictures which are closely integrated with the text.

Vocabulary   Very carefully restricted and graded.

Appraisal   This English scheme has been devised in such a way that the students using it have the happy experience of doing interesting work correctly from the start. There is little direct teaching of rules of usage as the author holds that children are more likely to learn written language skills by using them than by being drilled in them, and that the opportunity to use error-free English that is given by this type of planning inculcates good habits in the users. The material used in the books is pleasantly and interestingly presented. Although intended for children making normal progress, these books are suitable for use with slow learners, particularly poor readers, as their vocabulary is carefully restricted and closely related to that of most reading schemes.

Books on Social Studies and Science

It is useless to provide poor readers with special material for reading and English lessons and then expect them to cope with the normal class text-books for social studies and science. Yet this frequently happens, particular-ly in classes for slower learners in secondary schools.

The following list is an attempt to alleviate the situation a little. It is by no means comprehensive but gives a few suggestions about the type of suit-able material that is available at present and indicates the age-ranges with which it can be most profitably used. Little of the material suggested has been written especially for backward readers, but it has been chosen be-cause of its mature approach to the various subjects combined with simple language and attractive presentation. In most cases, books which take a concrete rather than an abstract approach have been preferred.

OUR BOOK CORNER   J. Wilson   (Chambers)

BOYS AND GIRLS	pp.	RA	IA	Price
First Shelf: six titles each	16	6—7	6—10	50p
Creatures of Colder Lands				per set
Animals of Warmer Lands				
Our Bird Friends				
Second Shelf: six titles each	16	6½—7½	6—10	50p
Farmyard Animals				per set
Children of Many Lands				
Things Men Have Learned				
Third Shelf: six titles each	16	7—8	7—12	50p
Men and Women at Work				per set
Children of Other Times				
Things We Eat and Drink				
Fourth Shelf: six titles each	16	7½—8½	7—12	50p
Useful Plants				per set
Travel				
Men, Animals and Other Creatures				

Covers   Printed and illustrated white linson; stitched backs; booklet size.

Printing   Excellent; clear 18pt. sans-serif type.

Illustrations   Beautifully reproduced pastel drawings in soft natural tones; eight full-page plates in each booklet.

Vocabulary   Very severely restricted and graded. Amount of reading limited to a few short sentences opposite each illustration.

Appraisal   Designed as supplementary material for use in infant schools, these delightful little books are acceptable to many retarded readers up to twelve years old. They provide excellent follow-up experiences for general science and early social studies lessons, and also provide valuable practice with words learnt in class vocabulary extension work.

Titles include:

The Polar Bear	The Robin	The Horse
Indian Children	The Giraffe	Counting
Rubber	The Wheel	Some Fruits

THE WORKING WORLD   Ed. S. S. Segal   (Cassell)

BOYS AND GIRLS	pp.	RA	IA	Price
First Year: fourteen titles	64	7—8	8—14	40p
Second Year: fourteen titles		8—9		
Third Year: nine titles		8½—9½	10—16	50p
Fourth Year: nine titles		9—10		

Covers   Coloured, printed, linen-faced paper-covered boards.

Printing   Good; 24pt. sans-serif type; spacious and arresting page layout.

Illustrations   One on almost every page, mainly printed in two-colour litho; choice of colour is a little harsh.

Vocabulary   Each of these books uses the basic three-hundred word vocabulary from 'Key Words to Literacy' (McNally and Murray, 1962), plus a limited number of special words carefully introduced within the text and listed at the end of each book.

Appraisal   This project is intended to provide for a four-year secondary school course for educationally sub-normal children. The idea has much to recommend it. The books are gay in appearance, use original material and have a down-to-earth approach to both subjects and pupils. They are not watered-down versions of conventional school texts but are designed especially for the limited abilities of their intended users, and the publishers and editor must be congratulated on their educational perspicacity in producing them. Each section is planned round a central theme—the home in the first year, employment in the fourth, for example. Each book takes a separate area, such as scripture, number, social studies or craftwork and relates it meaningfully to both the central theme and the pupil's everyday life. There has been much careful planning, so that all suggested activities and exercises are purposeful and involve the pupils in active learning experiences.

Although this amounts to an impressive collection of books, one cannot help wondering at times if the scheme is over-ambitious. There is a certain sameness about the books—uniform type face, similar illustrations and a constant editorial bias throughout. It seems likely that pupils may find this lack of variety stagnating and perhaps frustrating if they are confined to the series for several years.

Titles include:

First Year:	*Second Year:*
The Queen Has No Face	Working Out and About
Bible Homes	Two Plays
Third Year:	*Fourth Year:*
Safety on the Road	Ted's Transistor
Being a Citizen	Out at Work

READ ABOUT SCIENCE BOOKS   G. Stephenson   (Longmans)

BOYS	pp.	RA	IA	Price
Ten booklets	16	8–9	8–12	£1.20 per set

Covers   Coloured, illustrated card.

Printing   Good; 14pt. type; stimulating page layout.

Illustrations   Well-drawn and carefully planned pictures and diagrams printed in full colour, which elucidate many of the concepts introduced into the text.

Vocabulary   Restricted, with technical words kept to a minimum, and explained by diagrams.

Appraisal   Devised as an introduction to scientific principles for primary school children, these little books will be ideal for use with older pupils in ESN schools. Each takes an important topic such as light or gravity and gives a simple, concise, intelligible and accurate account of its most important qualities.

Titles include:

Stars and Planet	Atoms
Magnetism	Electricity

AS WE WERE H. G. Scarfe (Longmans)

BOYS AND GIRLS	pp.	RA	IA	Price
Twenty-four booklets	16	8–9	8–12	10p

Covers Coloured, illustrated card.

Printing Excellent; 14pt type; compact page layout which avoids an overcrowded appearance by careful placing of illustrations and well-spaced paragraphs.

Illustrations Printed in full-colour litho; the style of the pictures echoes that of the contemporary painters of the period described in each book.

Vocabulary Very simple sentence and paragraph structure.

Appraisal People make history, so it is appropriate that a series of books whose purpose is to introduce English history to quite young children should approach the task through the lives of people living at various periods up to five thousand years ago. These little picture books present vivid miniatures of English life in story form, with children as the main characters. The illustrations are perhaps the most valuable aspect of the series. As well as being beautiful to look at, they are packed with information and could well be a source of reference not only to young historians but to aspiring costume designers as well. Retarded children will look and then read with pleasure. A similar series of booklets from the same publishers, 'Famous Lives' by M. C. Borer, deals with significant figures in European history.

Titles include:

The Stone Age	An English Mediaeval House
A Monastery	The Railways

READ AND DISCOVER Various authors (Hulton Educational Press)

BOYS AND GIRLS	pp.	RA	IA	Price
Fifty titles	32	8–9	8–12	20p
Sixty-four activity cards				65p

Covers Illustrated paste-board with corners that rub rather badly in use; taped backs.

Printing Excellent; clear 18pt. type; imaginative layout with paragraphs clearly separated and illustrations placed in a variety of positions.

Illustrations Full-colour, two-colour and monochrome litho, with at least one picture on every page. Styles vary but all are attractive.

Vocabulary Restricted.

Appraisal Almost a scientific encyclopedia in minature, this series provides, in an attractive, economical manner, a wealth of factual reading. It makes excellent library material for the child who prefers fact to fiction and is also a good source of information for class projects in social studies and science.

Titles include:

Other People's Homes	Keeping Clean
Sending a Message	Rockets and Satellites

This complete series is available in boxed form under the title, *The Read and Discover Library of Information,* indexed for easy handling and accompanied by 64 *Activity Cards* for individual work. The complete library costs £9.75p.

CHILDREN FAR AND NEAR W. G. Moore (Hulton Educational Press)

BOYS AND GIRLS	pp.	RA	IA	Price
First Series: eight titles	24	8—9	8—12	21p each or £1.55p the set.
Second Series: eight titles	24	8—9	8—12	21p each or £1.55p the set
Making Far and Near Dolls (by Faith Eaton)	48	8—9	8—12	50p

Covers Brightly coloured and illustrated stiff card with taped backs.

Printing Good; clear 14pt. type and pleasing page layout.

Illustrations Bold, rather gaudily-coloured pictures; a half-page plate on every other page. The doll book has explanatory diagrams in black and white.

Vocabulary Restricted; simple sentence structure.

Appraisal These elementary social studies stories make good class text books for those older retarded readers who are interested in geography but are unable to cope with more orthodox books. The backgrounds of the stories are full of accurate yet picturesque detail.
'Making Far and Near Dolls' gives detailed but simple instructions for making rag dolls and dressing them in their national costumes, an activity ideally suited for a classroom project.

Titles include:

Pedro Drives the Llamas	Odak Hunts the Seal
Don Goes Down the Mine	Nicos Picks the Grapes

SCIENCE FROM THE BEGINNING B. L. Hampson & K. S. Evans (Oliver & Boyd)

BOYS AND GIRLS	pp.	RA	IA	Price
Book 1	80	8—9	8—12	40p
Book 2	80	8½—9½	8—12	
Book 3	80	9—10	9—14	
Book 4	80	9½—10½	9—14	

Teacher's Books available for each level, 75p—£1.00p each.

Covers Coloured, printed linson.

Printing Fair; 18pt. type in Book 1; 12pt. type in other books. Pages have an overcrowded appearance, mainly because of the unimaginative layout of the text.

Illustrations Several small, beautifully coloured pictures are packed on to each page in such a way that much of the careful design and informative detail tends to be overlooked.

Vocabulary Graded and slightly restricted.

Appraisal In spite of a rather low standard of layout, this remains a useful series. Covering a wide variety of scientific subjects, it is well thought out and provides a general science scheme which gives younger pupils and those with limited reading skill a solid basis for later, more detailed studies. The material is accurate and exciting, and the numerous activities suggested are both purposeful and practical.

STAR BOOK SERIES   Various authors   (Hamish Hamilton)

BOYS AND GIRLS	**pp.**	**RA**	**IA**	**Price**
Eight titles	32	8–9	9–14	30p
Workbooks	12			

Covers   Linson covered boards.

Printing   Books: 18pt bold sans-serif type with a well-spaced page layout. Workbooks: 14pt. sans-serif type with the exercises arranged so that there is adequate space for writing the answers.

Illustrations   Plenty of attractive pictures printed in three-colour process or in black and white. These are full of relevant detail which helps illuminate and expand the facts given in the text.

Vocabulary   Restricted.

Appraisal   Simple, well-written social studies texts are invaluable for use with slow-learning children, and this series, using as it does man's relationship with his environment as its major theme, provides a sound basis for the understanding of the primary problems of modern culture in relation to such subjects as food, housing and transport. The treatment is necessarily brief, but is at the same time thought-provoking. The workbooks are designed not only to test the pupils' comprehension of what has been read but also to encourage independent searching for further information, a process adding much to the value of the books.

Titles include: Man Needs Sun   Man Goes Fishing

JUNIOR SCIENCE SERIES   Various authors   (Frederick Muller)

BOYS AND GIRLS	**pp.**	**RA**	**IA**	**Price**
Twenty titles	64	9–10	9–14	75p

Covers   Cloth-covered boards.

Printing   Excellent; the books are printed in a mixture of type faces, the majority of the text being a clear 14pt. type. Carefully planned, spacious page layout.

Illustrations   These vary with the subjects of the books, but in the main, are clear photographs together with diagrams and sketches in two-colour litho.

Vocabulary   Slightly restricted; the inclusion of a rather heavy load of technical terms and unusual place names may hinder some weaker readers.

Appraisal   Simple, attractive books on scientific subjects are always welcome to teachers of older backward readers, provided, as this series does, that as well as being simple, they treat their subjects seriously and accurately. These books deal with such diverse subjects as penguins, aeroplanes and rock-collecting in a comprehensive fashion and suggest within the text many practical experiments and follow-up activities. They would be a useful addition to the class reference library and could also be used as the basis for a course of general science lessons with non-academic pupils.

Titles include:

Icebergs and Glaciers	Rock Collecting
Elephants	Magnets

ANIMALS OF THE WORLD SERIES   E. Osmond   (Oxford University Press)

BOYS AND GIRLS	RA	IA	Price
Two series	9–10	9–14	65p per Volume

Covers   Printed manilla.

Printing   Good; clear 10pt. type.

Illustrations   Numerous attractive black and white drawings and maps.

Vocabulary   Unrestricted; simple sentence structure.

Appraisal   Although a little difficult in some cases, these books make excellent nature study readers for older backward pupils. Each book gives a factual and very sympathetic account of the life and habits of a particular animal and also a good background account of the countries where it is found.

Titles include:

Elephants	Whales	Chamois
Camels	Chimpanzees	Reindeer

FOCUS BOOKS   N. F. Newbury   (Heinemann)

BOYS AND GIRLS	pp.	RA	IA	Price
Four titles	40	9–10	9–14	13p

Covers   Coloured card printed with photographs of children carrying out scientific experiments.

Printing   Excellent; a variety of type faces and sizes is used and the exciting layout draws on modern display techniques to achieve a decorative and tempting result.

Illustrations   A striking assortment of sketches, diagrams and cartoons, all printed in two-colour litho.

Vocabulary   Slightly restricted; a short glossary of technical terms is provided in each book.

Appraisal   Each book in this series concentrates on the characteristics and uses of a a familiar material or element and leads the reader to discover for himself some of the essential qualities of things he handles every day. Theory and practice are combined to give a sound introduction to scientific study. These books, although designed for use in primary schools, would be excellent as a basis for general science lessons with older retarded pupils.

Titles:

Focus on Glass	Focus on Fire
Focus on Rubber	Focus on Metals

DISCOVERING SCIENCE   D. H. Barratt   (E. J. Arnold)

BOYS AND GIRLS	pp.	RA	IA	Price
Eight titles	48	9–10	9–14	30p
Experimental cards for each title				43p per set

Covers Coloured linson printed with an appropriate design for each subject. The cards are conveniently packed in strong linson envelopes printed to match the book covers.

Printing Excellent; clear 12pt. type; diagrams and text are combined in the layout to form a coherent whole.

Vocabulary Slightly restricted; sentence structure is straightforward and commendably free from scientific jargon.

Appraisal Designed as an introductory course in physics for children in the upper grades of primary schools, this series would be ideal for use with slower learners in secondary schools. The emphasis throughout is on experimentation and concrete applications of scientific principles. The experiment cards are a convenient way to individualize instruction and encourage independent investigation.

Titles include:

Air	Electricity	Mechanics
Light	Sound	Heat

LEARNING SCIENCE G. Nunn (Ginn)

BOYS AND GIRLS	pp.	RA	IA	Price
Workbooks 1 & 2	48	9–10	9–14	18p
Workbooks 3 & 4	64	10–11	9–14	19p
Teaching Science	80			38p

Covers Printed paper.

Printing Good; 14pt. type; attractive layout but occasionally the space allowed for writing answers is inadequate.

Illustrations Black and white sketches and diagrams in appropriate positions throughout the text.

Vocabulary Slightly restricted; difficult words are explained by illustrations and diagrams.

Appraisal These well-designed workbooks form the basis of a general science course in which the pupil is put in the position of having to participate actively in every lesson, if he is to complete the tasks set him. Class experiments are suggested and are followed up by individual activities and stimulating written assignments. These workbooks would be particularly valuable for use with small groups of children in normal classes who are unable to keep up with the rest of the class. It would provide material at which they could work independently for some of the time that their brighter peers are doing more advanced work.

THE BASIC SCIENCE SERIES Ed. B. M. Parker (Wheaton)

BOYS AND GIRLS	pp.	RA	IA	Price
Forty-three titles	36	10–12	10–16	30p

Covers Beautifully illustrated, cloth-covered boards.

Printing Good; clear 14pt. type and interesting page layout.

Illustrations One on nearly every page; brightly coloured drawings arranged to form a frame for the text.

Vocabulary   Very little restriction but technical words kept to a minimum.

Appraisal   This series of short textbooks, dealing in an enlivening fashion with a wide variety of scientific subjects, is most useful with older backward pupils. It will serve to give them a general background of modern scientific thought expressed conscisely and clearly at an elementary level. It will also serve to broaden their knowledge of and interest in the world around them.

Titles include:

Matter, Molecules and Atoms	Satellites and Space Travel
Beyond the Solar System	Dependent Plants

SECTION 9

Books for the Teacher

Included in this section is a selection of books dealing generally with the psychology and education of slow-learning children, with language development, with the psychology and teaching of reading and with the diagnosis and treatment of specific difficulties. Teachers should find all these books of value in gaining insight into the difficulties of backward readers, and in gaining a better understanding of the reading process and the ways of diagnosing problems and organizing remedial help.

Baumeister, A. A. (ed.) *Mental Retardation, Appraisal, Education and Rehabilitation* Chicago, Aldine Publishing Co., 1967.
This rather long book makes a comprehensive survey of problems of mental retardation in the light of recent research findings. The chapters dealing with speech, language and hearing, learning abilities and programmed learning are of particular relevance to teachers.

Blair, G. M. *Diagnostic and Remedial Teaching* New York, Macmillan, 1956.
This book covers all the basic subjects, Part 1 dealing particularly with remedial teaching in reading. Organisation of remedial programmes in both primary and secondary schools is described, and valuable suggestions for classroom arrangements and remedial teaching procedures are described. There are frequent suggestions for supplementary apparatus and activities.

Bond, G. L. and Tinker, M. A. *Reading Difficulties: Their Diagnosis and Correction* New York: Appleton-Century-Crofts, 1957.
This American publication makes a comprehensive study of the principles of reading instruction, the causes and diagnosis of reading difficulties and their remedial treatment. The book is particularly useful in its detailed treatment of specific difficulties offering many practical suggestions for their alleviation which are comparatively simple for the classroom teacher to adapt to meet individual needs. Many interesting case studies are presented, showing the various types of difficulties and describing how the children were assisted in the light of their total need patterns.

Carlson, B. W. and Ginglend, D. R. *Play Activities for the Retarded Child* London, Cassell, 1962.
This book has nothing directly to do with the teaching of reading, but presents a series of activities designed to help the total development of severely and moderately retarded children. The authors' awareness of the needs of such children permeates the book. Many of the activities suggested would be excellent for use with younger children in ESN schools.

Chambers, A. *The Reluctant Reader* Oxford, Pergamon Press, 1969
Dealing with the problems of those who won't rather than of those who can't, this book is a serious analysis of the reading tastes of young people, mainly in non-academic high schools. The author has done considerable research into his subject and has many suggestions as to how children can be enticed into reading for sheer pleasure and on how to provide them with worth-while material that they will enjoy reading.

Cleugh, M. F. (ed.) *Teaching the Slow Learner:* Vol 1—*In the Special School;* Vol 2—*In the Primary School;* Vol 3—*In the Secondary School* London, Methuen, 1961.
These books recognize the problem that faces many teachers who are required, without specific training for the task, to teach slow-learning children. Each volume consists of a series of essays covering almost every aspect of the education of slow-learning children from the class-teacher's point of view. They are not psychological texts but practical handbooks. Each section has been written by a practising teacher and includes much good sense and many useful suggestions. Special attention is paid to the necessity of planning curricula particularly suited to the needs of subnormal children, and to the importance of expressional and social activities in contrast to rote learning of processes and skills.

Crawford, J. E. *Children with Subtle Perceptual-Motor Difficulties* Pittsburg, Stanwix House Inc., 1966.
Although in many ways an irritating book, this is still a useful explanation of the effects of minor cerebral dysfunction upon a child's learning ability and general

96

behaviour. Suggestions are made as to how to get help for such children and for their management in the classroom situation.

Dolch, E. W. *Teaching Reading in the Primary School* Champaigne, Ill., Garrard Press, 1950.
The late Edgar Dolch was one of the leading American investigators in the fields of reading and spelling. In this book, he made a simple analysis of the psychology of the reading process, examining in some detail the skills which are basic to effective reading, such as acquiring a sight vocabulary, learning phonics and using a basic reader. He also considered briefly the place of remedial teaching in the primary grades. Although in some ways outdated, this still remains a useful source book, with much in it of value to the class teacher.

Downing, J. *The Initial Teaching Alphabet* London, Cassell, 1962.
This book is a report of the progress that is being made in one of the most important experimental studies of reading being undertaken at the present time. It describes the development of the Initial Teaching Alphabet and the experimental programmes which are being carried out with it in primary schools. This is an important book which should be read by every reading teacher.

Ebersole, Marylou, Kephart, N. C. and Ebersole, J. B. *Steps to Achievement for the Slow Learner* Columbus, Ohio, Charles E. Merrill Publishing Co., 1968.
This book describes a method of teaching slow-learning children, especially those with some neurological damage, which uses motor activities as basic steps to achievement in a carefully planned pre-school programme. It emphasizes the necessity for adequate diagnosis and the careful planning of individual programmes.

Edwards, R. P. A. and Gibbon, V. *Words Your Children Use* London, Burke, 1964.
This list of words has been collected from the spontaneous writings of young children in primary schools in England. It is an excellent reference book for teachers preparing their own reading material.

Fernald, G. M. *Remedial Techniques in Basic School Subjects* New York, Macmillan, 1947.
This book remains one of the classics of remedial teaching. In Part 2, Fernald sets out her well-known and widely used method of helping very backward children to a fresh start in reading. It is based firstly on an interest approach and secondly (and more distinctively) on the use of kinaesthetic (mainly tracing) aids to learning.

Franklin, A. W. (ed.) *Word-Blindness or Specific Developmental Dyslexia* London, Pitman Medical Publishing Co., 1962.
This is a transcript of the proceedings of the London conference convened by the Invalid Children's Aid Society which resulted in the establishment of a Word Blind Committee to study the problems of children apparently suffering from this condition. It makes interesting reading and shows up sharply the differing opinions of psychologists and neurologists on the concept of dyslexia. It gives most remedial teachers a lot to think about.

Fries, C. C. *Linguistics and Reading* New York, Holt, Rinehart and Winston, 1963.
In this short book, Professor Fries suggests that the science of linguistics has much to offer those who are concerned mainly with the teaching of reading. His approach is not that of either a psychologist or a teacher and many of the applications that he suggests from his theoretical knowledge will seem naive to most teachers. But his analysis of the development of language and of reading skills from a linguistic point of view is extremely useful in pin-pointing exactly what we are trying to do when we endeavour to teach a child to read.

Gardner, K. *Towards Literacy* Oxford, Basil Blackwell, 1965.
A short statement of the author's view on the aims of teaching reading, this book emphasizes the idea that reading is a means of communication, not merely a system of decoding written symbols. It offers many suggestions for improving teaching techniques and for evaluating methods and materials.

Gates, A. I. *The Improvement of Reading* New York, Macmillan, 1947.
Over the past thirty years, Gates has been an outstanding figure among educational psychologists in America, his greatest achievements having been in connection with the psychology and teaching of reading. The above book, although published over twenty years ago, remains an important one in the field. All the major aspects are covered in a clear, down-to-earth manner which takes full account of research findings. This book is still of immense value to the teacher, not only increasing his theoretical knowledge of the psychology of reading and of methods of assessment and diagnosis of difficulties, but also because of the wealth of information it contains on classroom methods, apparatus and activities for helping both the beginner and the pupil in trouble over his reading. It remains an excellent reference book.

Holbrooke, D. *English for the Rejected: Training in Literacy in the Lower Streams of the Secondary School* Cambridge University Press, 1964.
Recognizing that not all children are suited for the traditional academic education provided by most secondary schools, the author makes an eloquent, if rather emotional, appeal for a fundamental reconsideration of the content of the curriculum, particularly in English and associated subjects, provided for slower learners. He points out that such children have their strengths and potentials which, however, will not come to fruition unless we 'develop an education based on a real acceptance of the nature of these children and their needs'. This is a thought-provoking book which has much to offer all teachers of retarded children.

Keeney, A. H. and Keeney, Virginia (eds.) *Dyslexia: Diagnosis and Treatment of Reading Disorders* St. Louis, C. B. Mosby Co., 1968.
This collection of papers presents the medical and neurological view of reading disability. It includes contributions from a variety of associated disciplines, including neurologists, opthalmologists, psychiatrists and speech pathologists and provides much information concerning the theory of minimal cerebral dysfunction and its effect upon learning. Ideas are put forward for treatment and management.

Kirk, A. S. *Educating Exceptional Children* New York, Houghton Mifflin, 1962.
The author of this book is pre-eminent in the field of exceptional children and he has written a workmanlike and carefully designed volume which compresses a tremendous amount of relevant material into a comparatively small space. It includes sections on children with exceptionally low or exceptionally high intelligence; on the various types of physically handicapped children and on children with sensory difficulties. Each chapter is succinctly summarized and is followed by a good bibliography and a series of discussion topics.

Lewis, M. M. *Language, Thought and Personality* New York, Basic Books Inc., 1963.
This is a clear and systematic account of the growth of language and its relationship to general intellectual and emotional development in infancy and childhood. It clarifies many of the problems that are faced by teachers and speech therapists treating children whose delay in acquiring language skills is slowing down their educational and social progress.

McLeod, J. (Ed.) *The Slow Learner in the Primary School* Sydney, Ian Novak, 1968.
The main purpose of this book is to summarize the philosophy, methods and research findings that characterized the Fred and Eleanor Schonell Educational Research Centre of the University of Queensland during the period when Dr. McLeod

was its deputy-director. It is a combination of theory and practice, a useful mixture well worth careful study by anyone involved with the education of retarded children. The major emphasis is on difficulties in learning to read.

Money, J. (ed.) *The Disabled Reader* Baltimore, Johns Hopkins Press, 1966.
A series of papers dealing with some recent research into the origins of severe reading problems and of the methods of dealing with them, this book is an important contribution to the literature. It will be particularly helpful for those teachers dealing with children with perceptual anomalies. It also has some useful critiques of popular methods of teaching reading.

Money, J. (ed.) *Reading Disability* Baltimore, Johns Hopkins Press, 1962.
This book, which is a report of a conference held in Baltimore on reading disabilities, consists of twelve papers by distinguished contributors from a variety of disciplines including neurology, psychology and education. It draws attention to much recent research that suggests that in future the approach to severe reading retardation is likely to be through linguistics and neurophysiology rather than through education and psychology as it has been in the past. Although many will disagree with its point of view, this book is a must for anyone working with children with severe reading disabilities.

Monroe, M. *Children Who Cannot Read* Chicago University Press, 1932.
Another classic in the field, this research monograph analyses the causal factors entering into reading disability and describes in detail a largely phonic approach to remedial teaching. It is one of the most widely cited publications in the literature and is worth looking at for its historical value alone.

Philips, I. (ed.) *Prevention and Treatment of Mental Retardation—An Interdisciplinary Approach to a Clinical Condition* New York, Basic Books Inc., 1966.
This is a comprehensive survey by a variety of experts into the modern approach to the problems of diagnosis, treatment and social implications of mental retardation. The section on 'Comprehensive Care of the Mentally Retarded' is of particular relevance to teachers of retarded children.

Ravenette, A. T. *Dimensions of Reading Difficulties* Oxford, Pergamon Press, 1968.
This short study summarizes the multiplicity of factors which contribute towards a child's failure to learn to read, into three major dimensions. It is a valuable book because it stresses the futility of looking for a single 'cause' for lack of progress and emphasizes the need for cognitive, social and neurological factors to be considered together when setting up a remedial programme.

Roswell, F. and Natchez, G. *Reading Disability: Diagnosis and Treatment* New York, Basic Books Inc., 1964.
This is an invaluable source of methods, hints and references for the newcomer to remedial teaching. The authors draw their material from their obviously long experience in this work and suggest detailed ways of improving word recognition, comprehension and study skills and also have much useful advice on the teaching of retarded and under-achieving pupils in secondary schools.

Russell, D. H. *Children Learn to Read* (rev. ed.) New York, Ginn, 1958.
Placing his emphasis on the theory of child development, the author of this rather unwieldy book attempts 'to examine research and good practice and apply these to reading problems in the modern elementary school.' In addition to the psychological, it covers sociological and historical backgrounds of reading. The reading programme is discussed in detail and the developmental phases in reading examined in a practical way.

Schonell, F. J. *The Psychology and Teaching of Reading* (4th. ed.) Edinburgh,
Oliver and Boyd, 1961.
First published in 1945, this comparatively short book has probably been more
widely used by teachers and parents than any other six publications on reading. In
exposition, it is a model of conciseness and clarity; its theory is based firmly on the
author's own research. It appeals to the teacher with its sound, practical common-
sense on what can and what cannot be done in the classroom. Coverage includes a
psychological analysis of reading methods, reading readiness, organization of reading in infant and junior schools, a description of a graded word vocabulary test,
suggestions for reading exercises and methods and materials for older pupils.

Schonell, F. J. *Backwardness in the Basic Subjects* Edinburgh, Oliver and Boyd,
1948.
This book remains a standard work of reference in the United Kingdom and other
Commonwealth countries. It covers backwardness in the related subjects of reading, spelling, oral and written English. Based on the late Sir Fred Schonell's own
extensive research, it gives teachers, in clear, concise prose, an account of the
psychology of learning as it can be applied to these basic subjects. It analyses the
difficulties that pupils encounter in the primary school and gives details of diagnostic procedures and suggestions for remediation. Written by a man who knew the
problems of teachers at first hand, the book's outstanding feature is its realism and
practicability. The measures advocated are sound theoretically and have been shown
to work in the classroom.

Schonell, F. J. and Schonell, F. E. *Diagnostic and Attainment Testing* (4th. ed.)
Edinburgh, Oliver and Boyd, 1962.
The two functions of this book are to give teachers guidance in the use and interpretation of objective attainment tests and to bring together in a convenient form
all the authors' diagnostic and attainment tests. Tests included cover reading, spelling,
arithmetic, diagnostic English and written composition. Two brief final chapters list
remedial materials for backward pupils and books for professional reading.

Segal, S. S. *11+ Rejects* London. The Schoolmaster Press, 1961.
This short book sets out, in a practical fashion based on the author's own experience,
the procedures necessary for selecting suitable children and setting up a remedial class
in a secondary school. It covers choice of curricula, social training through the dele-
gation of responsibility, and the effectiveness of remedial techniques. This book is
particularly valuable to secondary school teachers who have had no previous experience in this type of work.

Segal, S. S. *Teaching Backward Pupils* London, Evans Brothers, 1963.
A useful handbook for teachers of retarded children, this book surveys the nature
of the problems such teachers have to face and discusses the aims and methods the
author considers most suitable and most likely to lead to the maximum development of the less academically favoured child. Each area of the curriculum is discussed in detail and the author has many ideas for improving teaching techniques
and making the job more satisfying for the teacher.

Smith, J. O. *Effects of a Group Language Development Programme Upon the
Psycholinguistic Abilities of Educable Mental Retardates* Nashville, Tennessee,
George Peabody College for Teachers, 1962.
This research monograph describes in detail the effect of a carefully planned language
development programme on the general educational progress of a group of mildly
retarded (ESN) children. It presents evidence of the general need for such programmes
and of the usefulness of the Illinois Test of Psycholinguistic Abilities in assessing
language abilities and improvement in such children. It also gives in detail the experimental programme used.

Smith, N. B. *Reading Instruction for Today's Children* New York, Prentice-Hall, 1963. This very long book covers a wide variety of subjects associated with the teaching of reading and is a most useful reference book. The author gives a historical survey of methods of teaching reading used in America, reviews the psychological background, and studies in detail the various methods and techniques of teaching reading.

Southgate, Vera and Roberts, G. R. *Reading—Which Approach?* London, University of London Press, 1970.
The authors' main aim for this book is to help teachers choose the best reading scheme to suit the needs of the children they are going to teach and the one which best suits their individual philosophy and method of education. Criteria for assessing reading approaches are discussed in detail and nine approaches to reading currently used in the United Kingdom are critically examined.

Tarnapol, L. (ed.) *Learning Disabilities: Introduction to Educational and Medical Management* Springfield, U.S.A. Charles C. Thomas, 1969.
This book deals with the problems of children with minimal cerebral dysfunction and discusses in detail diagnosis, treatment and the organisation of special educational programmes for such children. Much recent research is cited and recent methods of treatment are critically appreciated.

Tansley, A. E. *Reading and Remedial Reading* London, Routledge and Kegan Paul, 1967.
This book discusses in simple terms both the theoretical and practical aspects of teaching reading. It describes in detail the author's diagnostic procedures and remedial treatment of neurologically damaged children with severe reading difficulties, the methods described being derived from the author's experience with children in a Birmingham (England) special school. This is an outstanding contribution to the literature of reading retardation and essential reading for anyone dealing with children with severe reading difficulties.

The Slow Learning Child University of Queensland Press, Australia. Thrice Yearly.
This journal, which deals with the education of backward children and originates from the Fred and Eleanor Schonell Educational Research Centre of the University of Queensland, includes articles on both theoretical and practical issues in the education of retarded children. It also reviews regularly new books for retarded readers.

Vernon, M. D. *Backwardness in Reading, A Study of Its Nature and Origin* Cambridge University Press, 1957.
This scholarly summary and appraisal of the large volume of research into the causal factors in reading backwardness is now a little out-of-date but still remains of great value to all those concerned with this problem either in the classroom, in teacher training or in research. It examines the association between perception and reading success, clarifies the position on many theoretical aspects of reading backwardness, removes some misconceptions and brings out clearly the implications of research in the classroom.

24 POINT
GILL MEDIUM

THE SIZE OF the type face is also included so that the teacher can get some idea of the appear

24 POINT
BASKERVILLE

THE SIZE OF the type face is also included so that the teacher can get some idea of the appear

24 POINT
CENTURY
SCHOOLBOOK

THE SIZE OF the type face is also included so that the teacher can get some

24 POINT
UNIVERS
MEDIUM

THE SIZE OF the type face is also included so that the teacher can get some

THE SIZE OF the type face is also included so that the teacher can get some idea of the appearance of the pages.

THE SIZE OF the type face is also included so that the teacher can get some idea of the appearance of the pages. Examples of four popular

THE SIZE OF the type face is also included so that the teacher can get some idea of the appearance of the pages.

THE SIZE OF the type face is also included so that the teacher can get some idea of the appearance of the

THE SIZE OF the type face is also included so that the teacher can get some idea of the appearance of the pages. Examples of four popular faces that have proved suitable for

THE SIZE OF the type face is also included so that the teacher can get some idea of the appearance of the pages. Examples of four popular faces that have

14 POINT
CENTURY
SCHOOLBOOK

THE SIZE OF the type face is also included so that the teacher can get some idea of the appearance of the pages. Examples of four popular

14 POINT
UNIVERS
MEDIUM

THE SIZE OF the type face is also included so that the teacher can get some idea of the appearance of the pages. Examples of four

12 POINT
GILL MEDIUM

THE SIZE OF the type face is also included so that the teacher can get some idea of the appearance of the pages. Examples of four popular faces that have proved suitable for

12 POINT
BASKERVILLE

THE SIZE OF the type face is also included so that the teacher can get some idea of the appearance of the pages. Examples of four popular faces that have proved suitable for

12 POINT
CENTURY
SCHOOLBOOK

THE SIZE OF the type face is also included so that the teacher can get some idea of the appearance of the pages. Examples of four popular faces that have proved suitable for

12 POINT
UNIVERS
MEDIUM

THE SIZE OF the type face is also included so that the teacher can get some idea of the appearance of the pages. Examples of four popular faces that have

10 POINT GILL MEDIUM

THE SIZE OF the type face is also included so that the teacher can get some idea of the appearance of the pages. Examples of four popular faces that have proved suitable for educational use are shown here.

10 POINT BASKERVILLE

THE SIZE OF the type face is also included so that the teacher can get some idea of the appearance of the pages. Examples of four popular faces that have proved suitable for educational use are shown here.

10 POINT CENTURY SCHOOLBOOK

THE SIZE OF the type face is also included so that the teacher can get some idea of the appearance of the pages. Examples of four popular faces that have proved suitable for educational use are shown here.

10 POINT UNIVERS MEDIUM

THE SIZE OF the type face is also included so that the teacher can get some idea of the appearance of the pages. Examples of four popular faces that have proved suitable for

8 POINT GILL MEDIUM

THE SIZE OF the type face is also included so that the teacher can get some idea of the appearance of the pages. Examples of four popular faces that have proved suitable for educational use are shown here.

8 POINT BASKERVILLE

THE SIZE OF the type face is also included so that the teacher can get some idea of the appearance of the pages. Examples of four popular faces that have proved suitable for educational use are shown here.

8 POINT CENTURY SCHOOLBOOK

THE SIZE OF the type face is also included so that the teacher can get some idea of the appearance of the pages. Examples of four popular faces that have proved suitable for educational use are shown here.

8 POINT UNIVERS MEDIUM

THE SIZE OF the type face is also included so that the teacher can get some idea of the appearance of the pages. Examples of four popular faces that have proved suitable for educational use are shown here.

Index

Famous Ships: Brookfield, Newton & Smith, 76
Far and Near Readers: various authors, 44
Fifteen: ed. M. Grieve, 78
First Steps in Reading for Meaning: G. Carr, 81
Flamingo Books: various authors, 62
Focus Books: N. F. Newbury, 91
Fountain Picture Books: J. Brandon & D. Norris, 50

Ginger Books: K. C. Briand, 53
Go Readers: M. Calman, 43
Griffin Pirate Stories: S. K. McCullagh, 52

Happy Venture Books: F. J. Schonell, I. Serjeant & P. Flowerdew, 50
Help Yourself Handwork: H. E. Manistre, 75

Inner Ring Books: A. Pullen, C. Rapstoff and Michael Hardcastle, 45

Jets: various authors, 67
Joan Tate Books: J. Tate, 68
Junior Reading Series: various authors, 62
Junior Science Series: various authors, 90

Kennett Library: ed. J. Kennett, 69

Learning Science: G. Nunn, 92
Longman's Structural Readers: various authors, 36
Lookout Gang: M. B. Chapman, 42

McKee Readers: P. McKee et al., 51
Measuring and Making: C. Carver and C. H. Stowasser, 75
Mike and Mandy Readers: M. Durward, 54

New Reading: ed. A. E. Scott, 34

Our Book Corner: J. Wilson, 86
Oxford Colour Books: C. Carver and C. H. Stowasser, 30
Oxford Junior Workbooks: C. Carver and C. H. Stowasser, 30

Pathfinder Books: J. and P. Bradley, 31

Read About Science: ed. K. Gardner, 77
Read About Science Books: G. Stephenson, 87

Section 9

Printed in Great Britain by
Unwin Brothers Limited
THE GRESHAM PRESS   OLD WOKING   SURREY   ENGLAND